REAL BRITISH DISHES

By the same author

Real Soups & Sauces
The Barbecue Cook
Microwave Cooking Times At A Glance!
The Combination Microwave Cook
Microwave Cooking Properly Explained
The Microwave Planner
Microwave Recipes For One

Uniform with this book

REAL BRITISH DISHES

Annette Yates

RIGHT WAY

Typeset in 10/11pt Times by Letterpart Ltd., Reigate, Surrey.
Printed and bound in Great Britain by Cox & Wyman Ltd., Reading, Berkshire.

The *Right Way* series is published by Elliot Right Way Books, Brighton Road, Lower Kingswood, Tadworth, Surrey, KT20 6TD, U.K. For information about our company and the other books we publish, visit our web site at **www.right-way.co.uk**

CONTENTS

Illustrations by
Lindsay Thomas

INTRODUCTION

This book is a celebration of British dishes, in which the foreign and the exotic are put aside in favour of the traditional and the familiar. I have gathered together this collection of recipes from England, Wales, Scotland and Ireland. Though it is by no means exhaustive (undoubtedly, each of you will have many regional recipes that you could add to it), these are the ones that I have enjoyed making for family and friends over the years. In them, I hope to have represented each part of the British Isles with some of its most famous traditional dishes. They are recipes that can be traced back into history. With this in mind, I have accompanied each one with what I think is an interesting anecdote – it may be historical, geographical or religious, or simply a tip on how to vary the recipe. When I felt it was appropriate, I have brought recipes up to date by using up-to-the-minute ingredients and modern (quick) methods.

This book also provides me with an opportunity to extol the virtues of British foods and British seasons. These days, we are able to buy foods from all over the world at any time of the year.

7

"Wonderful!" you may say but, by having (fairly tasteless) strawberries and asparagus in the winter months, have we lost touch with the British seasons? It seems there is now a distinct lack of knowledge about British seasonal foods – research has shown that most of us know that 'food in season' is good, but many of us have little idea of when those seasons occur. Maybe we are also losing touch with how food should really taste? When we are able to buy strawberries all year round, can our enthusiasm possibly be so great at the approach of the British strawberry season with its wonderful influx of colour and, above all, flavour? British farmers are finding it harder and harder to survive. We can help by rediscovering the pleasures of eating locally-produced food when it is in season. Many farms are returning to rearing and growing organic food and they believe that, with fruit and vegetables left to grow to their optimum ripeness and with short transportation distances, their foods have better nutrition and greatly improved flavour. With science developing so quickly, increasingly we the consumers want to know where our food comes from. One way is to recognise and look forward to the seasons – just like we used to years ago.

Finally, I would like to record my sincere thanks to the following individuals and companies for their help and support in gathering together the recipes for this book: *Marguerite Patten OBE* for her generous advice, *Margaret Howard, Denman College (The National Federation of Women's Institutes)* for allowing me to delve into the College's collection of historical cookery books, hand-written notebooks and scrapbooks, *Sue Batty, Van den Bergh Foods*, and *Jennifer John and The British Potato Council*. As usual, my family and friends have been wonderful, offering me their handed-down-the-family recipes, testing and tasting the recipes in this book and providing me with their honest opinions. Thanks to everyone!

Now, get cooking and rediscover and enjoy these real British dishes.

Annette Yates

1

ABOUT THE RECIPES

Serving suggestions and recipe variations: when these are appropriate, they are included in the anecdote.

Servings: most recipes serve 4 or more, since I feel sure you will want to serve them at gatherings of family and/or friends.

Ingredient measurements: for best results, use one set only – metric or imperial. In general, you may find the metric measurements easier to use.

Spoon measurements: these are level, unless otherwise stated.

Eggs used are medium, unless otherwise stated. Some recipes may contain raw or partially-cooked eggs. Do remember that it is not advisable to serve these to pregnant women, the very young, the elderly or the sick.

Recipe methods: where possible, I have tried to bring traditional methods up to date, to fit in with today's busy lifestyles. You will see that I often use ingredients such as ready-made puff pastry and canned beans. If you have the time, or if you prefer, there is no reason why you should not make your own pastry or soak and cook dried beans. These recipes are not meant to be 'written in stone', the choice is always yours.

Stock: home-made is best of course, but cartons and bottles of fresh stock (sometimes concentrated) are available, which are very good and contain little salt, sugar or artificial additives. I also keep a supply of my favourite stock cubes and granules in the store-cupboard – some of them are really quite good and they are handy when I am in a hurry.

Microwave methods: when a recipe is appropriate, and many are, the microwave method has been provided. These recipes have been tested in a microwave oven with a wattage of 700-800W. If your microwave has a lower wattage, you will need to cook for a little longer. If it has a higher wattage, then simply lower the power level slightly and cook for the time given in the recipe.

All cooking is on HIGH (700-800W) unless otherwise stated. MED-HIGH is equivalent to 500-600W, MEDIUM is 350-400W and MED-LOW is 200-300W.

You will notice that, particularly when making soups, I often use *hot* stock to speed up cooking (so if you make up a stock cube or granules, dissolve it/them in boiling water from the kettle, then add the hot liquid to the recipe).

Combination microwave ovens: space has prevented me from providing methods for these excellent cookers. However, those of you who use combination ovens on a regular basis will know that some of the recipes in this book – particularly roast dishes, pies, cakes and bakes – will be suitable. Please check with your manufacturer's instruction/recipe book and, if possible, use a similar recipe as your guide.

For information on microwave or combination cooking, please write to me, enclosing a stamped, self-addressed envelope, at Microwave Cook, Pine Trees, Church Road, Earsham NR35 2TJ.

2

SOUPS, STARTERS, SNACKS & LIGHT MEALS

Whether you need a bowl of warming soup, a starter course for dinner, or a snack, lunch or supper dish, this is the section to look in. Make a dish as substantial as you like by accompanying it with bread, biscuits or salads, whichever is the most appropriate for the recipe and the occasion. Just one recipe – Pease Pudding – may not seem to slot into this chapter but, rather than omit it, I have included it here.

Cock-a-Leekie Soup

Chicken and leeks provide the main ingredients for this Scottish broth. Originally, a whole bird would have been cooked in the broth (some for the soup and some for another use) and a little beef added too. The recipe below uses chicken portions. To be authentic, it includes rice, though a more modern version would probably contain prunes – the choice is yours.

Serves 4

350g/12 oz leeks
25g/1 oz butter
1 large or two small chicken portion(s), total weight about
   350g/12 oz
1 litre/1¾ pt chicken stock
bouquet garni
salt and freshly ground black pepper
25g/1 oz rice (preferably a medium grain, such as risotto rice), OR
   8 ready-to-eat dried prunes, each quartered
2 tbsp finely chopped fresh parsley

1. Thinly slice the white parts of the leeks, reserving the green parts.

2. Melt the butter in a large pan and brown the chicken on all sides. Add the white leeks and cook gently for about 5 minutes, stirring occasionally, until beginning to soften.

3. Add the stock, bouquet garni and seasoning. Bring to the boil, then cover and simmer gently for about 30 minutes or until the chicken is very tender.

4. Lift out the chicken and cut the meat into small pieces, discarding skin and bones.

5. Thinly slice the reserved green leeks and add to the pan with the chicken and rice (or prunes). Bring to the boil, cover and simmer gently for about 15 minutes.

6. Stir in the parsley just before serving.

To microwave:

1. Thinly slice the white parts of the leeks, reserving the green parts.

2. Put the butter and white leeks into a large casserole, cover and cook on HIGH for about 3 minutes until soft.

3. Add the chicken, half the *hot* stock, bouquet garni and seasoning. Cover and cook on HIGH for about 5 minutes or until the mixture comes to the boil. Continue cooking on MEDIUM for about 15 minutes or until the chicken is very tender.

4. Lift out the chicken and cut the meat into small pieces, discarding skin and bones.

5. Thinly slice the reserved green leeks and add to the casserole with the chicken, rice (or prunes) and the remaining *hot* stock. Cover and cook on HIGH for about 5 minutes or until the soup comes to the boil. Continue cooking on MEDIUM for about 10 minutes.

6. Stir in the parsley just before serving.

Potato Soup with Parsley or Nutmeg

I am told that it was once an Irish custom to keep a potato in your pocket – to cure rheumatism. Cure or not, the Irish have provided us with a wealth of delicious and economical dishes using potatoes as their main ingredient. This is one of them. Use a British-grown floury variety such as King Edward or Desirée. Sometimes, a couple of streaky bacon rashers are chopped up and crisp-cooked in the butter first. I like to serve the soup topped with some crunchy croûtons, made by browning some small cubes of bread in butter or oil.

Serves 4-6

25g/1 oz butter
1 medium onion, thinly sliced
550g/1¼ lb potatoes, peeled and sliced
700ml/1¼ pt chicken or vegetable stock
salt and freshly ground pepper
300ml/½ pt milk
¼ tsp grated nutmeg or 3 tbsp finely chopped fresh parsley
3 tbsp double cream (optional)

1. Melt the butter in a pan and add the onion and potatoes. Cook gently for about 10 minutes, stirring occasionally, without browning.

2. Add the stock and seasoning. Bring to the boil, cover and simmer gently for 20-25 minutes until the vegetables are very soft.

3. Either pass the soup through a sieve or tip into a food processor or blender and purée until smooth.

4. Return the soup to the pan and stir in the milk and nutmeg or parsley. Bring to the boil then simmer gently for 5 minutes.

5. Stir in the cream, if using, just before serving.

To microwave:

1. Put the butter, onion and potatoes into a large casserole. Cover and cook on HIGH for 5 minutes, stirring once.

2. Add half the *hot* stock and the seasoning. Cover and cook on HIGH for about 15 minutes, stirring once or twice, until the vegetables are very soft.

3. Add the remaining *hot* stock. Either pass the soup through a sieve or tip into a food processor or blender and purée until smooth.

4. Return the soup to the casserole and stir in the milk and nutmeg or parsley. Cook on HIGH for 5 minutes, stirring once.

5. Stir in the cream, if using, just before serving.

Leek Soup

Cawl Cennin is the Welsh name for this dish, whose main ingredient is the leek – the national emblem of Wales. Years ago, it would have made a two-course meal – the cawl, or broth, thickened with oatmeal, would have been served first, followed by the bacon and vegetables. The recipe below uses flour as a thickener and, to shorten the cooking time, rashers in place of a large piece of bacon. Serve it as a starter or as a main dish with crusty bread and a hunk of well-flavoured British cheese.

Serves 4

25g/1 oz butter
4 bacon rashers, rinds removed and finely chopped
1 medium carrot, finely chopped
1 medium main-crop potato, peeled and thinly sliced
1½ tbsp flour
850ml/1½ pt chicken or vegetable stock
450g/1 lb leeks, thinly sliced
salt and freshly ground black pepper
finely chopped fresh parsley or snipped chives

1. Melt the butter in a large pan, add the bacon and cook over medium heat for a few minutes, stirring occasionally, until just beginning to brown. Add the carrot and potato and cook, stirring occasionally, for 5-10 minutes or until the vegetables begin to soften without browning.

2. Stir in the flour. Remove from the heat and gradually stir in the stock. Add the leeks and a little seasoning.

3. Bring to the boil, stirring. Cover and simmer gently for about 30 minutes until the vegetables are tender.

4. Adjust seasoning to taste. Serve, topped with parsley or chives.

To microwave:

1. Put the butter into a large casserole and add the bacon, carrot and potato. Cover and cook on HIGH for about 5 minutes, stirring occasionally, until the vegetables begin to soften.

2. Stir in the flour then gradually stir in half the *hot* stock. Add the leeks and a little seasoning.

3. Cover and cook on HIGH for about 15 minutes, stirring once or twice, until the vegetables are very soft.

4. Add the remaining *hot* stock and adjust seasoning to taste. Serve, topped with parsley or chives.

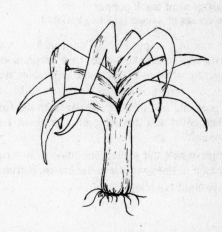

Pea Soup or London Particular

In the 1800s, London was regularly shrouded in thick winter fog – called a pea-souper or London Particular because it resembled the colour and consistency of pea soup. The original recipe would have been made with pig's trotters and, perhaps, a marrow bone. Serve this updated version topped with croûtons and small pieces of crisp-cooked bacon.

Serves 4

15g/½ oz butter
25g/1 oz lean streaky bacon, rind removed and finely chopped
1 small onion, finely chopped
1 small carrot, thinly sliced
1 small celery stick, thinly sliced
225g/8 oz split dried green peas, soaked overnight in plenty of cold water
1.2 litre/2 pt ham or chicken stock
salt and freshly ground black pepper
4 tbsp double cream or crème fraîche (optional)

1. Heat the butter in a large saucepan until melted. Add the bacon, onion, carrot and celery and cook over medium heat for 5-10 minutes, stirring occasionally until the vegetables are soft but not brown.

2. Drain the peas and add them to the pan with the stock. Bring to the boil, then cover and simmer gently for about 1 hour or until the peas are soft.

3. Tip into a processor and purée until smooth. Return the soup to the pan, season to taste and stir in the cream, if using.

4. Heat through until bubbling.

To microwave:

1. Put the butter in a large casserole and add the bacon, onion, carrot and celery. Cover and cook on HIGH for 5 minutes, stirring once, until the vegetables are soft.

2. Drain the peas and add them to the casserole with the *hot* stock. Cook on HIGH for 5-10 minutes or until the mixture comes to the boil, then cook, uncovered, on HIGH for 10 minutes. Cover and continue cooking on MED-LOW for about 30 minutes or until the peas are soft.

3. Tip into a processor and purée until smooth. Return the soup to the casserole, season to taste and stir in the cream, if using.

4. Heat on HIGH, stirring once, until just bubbling.

Scotch Broth

Scotland's most famous soup makes a meal in itself. Originally it would have contained neck of mutton or shin of beef and, when they were in season, peas and cabbage. By using lamb cutlets and lamb stock, I have been able to reduce the cooking time by at least one hour. Remember that turnip in Scotland is known as swede in the South.

Serve 6

1 tbsp oil
6 lean best-end-neck lamb cutlets, trimmed of excess fat
1 large onion, finely chopped
1 large carrot, finely chopped
about 175g/6 oz turnip (see note) or swede
2 medium leeks, thinly sliced
4 tbsp pearl barley
1.2 litre/2 pt lamb stock
300ml/½ pt vegetable stock
salt and freshly ground black pepper
4 tbsp chopped fresh parsley

1. Heat the oil in a large pan and quickly brown the lamb on all sides. Lift out.

2. Add the vegetables and barley to the pan and cook over medium heat, stirring occasionally, for about 5 minutes until the vegetables begin to soften without browning.

3. Return the lamb to the pan and add the lamb and vegetable stock. Bring to the boil, then cover and simmer gently for 40 minutes or until the barley is soft.

4. Season to taste and stir in the parsley.

To microwave:

1. On the hob, heat the oil in a frying pan and quickly brown the lamb on all sides.

2. Put the vegetables and barley into a large casserole, cover and cook on HIGH for 5 minutes, stirring once.

3. Add the lamb with the sediment from the pan and half the *hot* stock. Cook on HIGH for about 5 minutes or until the mixture comes to the boil. Cover and cook on MED-LOW for 40 minutes or until the barley is soft.

4. Stir in the remaining *hot* stock, season to taste and stir in the parsley.

Mulligatawny

The term Mulligatawny comes from the Tamil words for pepper and water. There are many versions of this mildly-spiced dish, created in the days of the British Raj, when cooks in Southern India prepared it for their British sahibs. The recipe below is currently my favourite. Sometimes I replace the cooking apple with a diced fresh mango, added about 5 minutes before the end of cooking. Use mild, medium or hot curry powder, according to taste. Naan bread or chappatis make the ideal accompaniment.

Serves 4

25g/1 oz butter or ghee
1 large onion, thinly sliced
1 medium carrot, finely chopped
2 medium celery sticks, thinly sliced
1 plump garlic clove, finely chopped
2 tbsp flour
2 tsp curry powder
1.2 litre/2 pt chicken stock
1 large cooking apple
2 tsp lemon juice
25g/1 oz basmati rice
25-55g/1-2 oz cooked chicken meat, cut into shreds
salt and freshly milled pepper
4 tbsp single cream
2 tbsp fresh coriander leaves, roughly chopped

1. Melt the butter or ghee in a pan and stir in the onion, carrot, celery and garlic. Cook gently for about 10 minutes, stirring occasionally, until soft but not brown.

2. Stir in the flour and curry powder. Cook, stirring, for 2-3 minutes. Gradually blend in the stock and cook, stirring, until the mixture comes to the boil and thickens slightly. Cover and simmer gently for 30 minutes, stirring occasionally.

3. Peel, core and dice the apple and add to the pan with the lemon juice, rice and chicken. Season with salt and pepper.

4. Cover and simmer gently for about 15 minutes, or until the rice is tender.

5. Remove from the heat and leave to cool slightly. Stir in the cream and coriander and serve.

To microwave:

1. Put the butter, onion, carrot, celery and garlic into a large casserole. Cover and cook on HIGH for about 5 minutes, stirring once or twice, until soft.

2. Stir in the flour and curry powder and cook, uncovered, for 1 minute. Gradually blend in half the *hot* stock. Cook on HIGH for about 4 minutes, stirring once or twice, until the mixture comes to the boil. Cover and cook on MEDIUM for 6 minutes.

3. Peel, core and dice the apple and add to the casserole with the lemon juice, rice and chicken. Season with salt and pepper.

4. Add the remaining *hot* stock. Cover and cook on HIGH for about 10 minutes or until the rice is just tender. If time allows, leave the soup to stand, covered, for 10 minutes.

5. Stir in the cream and coriander and serve.

Cullen Skink

Cullen is a village on the edge of the Moray Firth in Scotland; skink is supposed to mean broth or stock. Finnan haddock is traditional in this area and, with potatoes, is a main ingredient of this substantial soup. If you cannot get Finnan haddock, use any smoked haddock (though not the dyed yellow sort). I have left the potatoes in pieces, but many Scots prefer to mash them.

Serves 4 for lunch or 6 as a starter

450g/1 lb potatoes, peeled and thinly sliced
salt and freshly ground pepper
25g/1 oz butter
1 medium onion, finely chopped
450g/1 lb Finnan or other smoked haddock
600ml/1 pt vegetable stock
300ml/½ pt milk
150ml/¼ pt double cream (optional)
chopped fresh parsley, to serve

1. Cook the potatoes in boiling, salted water for about 20 minutes until tender.

2. Meanwhile, melt the butter in a frying pan and add the onion. Cook over medium heat for 5-10 minutes, stirring occasionally, until soft but not brown. Add the fish and pour the stock over. Heat until the liquid just bubbles, then cover and cook gently for about 10 minutes until the fish is just cooked.

3. Lift the fish from the pan, reserving the liquid and onion. Flake the fish roughly, discarding skin and bones.

4. Drain the potatoes and return them to the rinsed pan. Add the flaked fish and the reserved liquid and onion. Stir in the milk and season to taste.

5. Heat gently until the soup just bubbles. Stir in the cream, if using, and serve, topped with parsley.

To microwave:

1. Put the butter and onion into a dish large enough to hold the fish in one layer. Cover and cook on HIGH for 3-5 minutes, stirring once, until soft. Lay the haddock on top and pour over three-quarters of the *hot* stock. Cover and cook on HIGH for 5 minutes. Leave to stand, covered.

2. Meanwhile, put the potatoes into a large casserole with the remaining stock. Cover and cook on HIGH for 8-10 minutes, stirring once or twice, until tender.

3. Lift the fish from the dish, reserving the liquid and onion. Flake the fish roughly, discarding skin and bones.

4. Add the fish to the potatoes in the casserole. Stir in the reserved liquid and onion. Add the milk and season to taste.

5. Heat on MEDIUM, stirring once, until just bubbling.

Kipper Pâté

Kippers, or smoked herrings, are a speciality of Scotland, Northumbria, East Anglia and the Isle of Man. Kipper pâté is a favourite starter in my family. For the best flavour use kippers from your favourite supplier and cook them gently in butter. The recipe below uses chilled or frozen boil-in-the-bag varieties. It is also suitable for smoked mackerel fillets – simply remove their skins, flake the flesh and skip straight to step 3. Serve it with fresh crusty bread or with crisp hot toast.

Serves 4

200g chilled or frozen boned kipper fillets with butter
4 tbsp crème fraîche, thick Greek-style yogurt or double cream
good squeeze of fresh lemon juice
1-2 tsp horseradish sauce
freshly ground black pepper
chopped fresh parsley or dill, to serve

1. Cook the kippers following the packet instructions (for microwaving, remember to pierce the bag).

2. Leave to cool slightly, then cut the bag and let the fish and its juices slide out on to a plate. Remove and discard the skin.

3. For a smooth pâté, put the fish and its juices into a processor, add the crème fraîche, lemon juice and horseradish sauce and purée until smooth. For a rougher pâté, put the ingredients into a bowl and mix until combined. Season to taste with pepper, adding extra lemon juice if you wish.

4. Spoon into one large dish or four small ones. Cover and chill for at least 2 hours.

5. Serve, garnished with parsley or dill.

Potted Cheese

As far back as the 17th century, potting was a method used to preserve foods like cheese, meat and fish. Today, it's a good way of using cheese that is likely to sit in the fridge for longer than necessary. It makes a good sandwich filling or a snack, served with crusty bread or crisp biscuits. This recipe includes the traditional flavouring of mace and cayenne, but you could replace these with curry powder or a tablespoon of chopped fresh herbs, such as chives, mint or parsley. This version is left plain, but a topping of butter (melted before pouring over and leaving to set) looks particularly attractive.

Serves 4-6

85g/3 oz butter, softened
225g/8 oz grated British cheese, such as Cheshire, Cheddar or
  Stilton
½ tsp ground mace
pinch of cayenne
about 2 tbsp sherry or port (use the latter with Stilton)
freshly ground pepper

1. Put all the ingredients into a bowl and beat well, adding a little extra sherry or port if necessary to make a smooth consistency.

2. Spoon into one large dish or several small ones. Cover and chill for at least 2 hours.

Potted Meat

Potting meat with spices was, and still is, a good way of using leftover roast meat. The original version would have used mace and cayenne as flavourings. I use freshly grated nutmeg and, sometimes, a dash of Worcestershire sauce. An elderly friend of mine likes to eat Potted Meat for breakfast, spread on hot toast. It's also ideal for filling sandwiches or for serving as a snack with crusty bread or crisp plain biscuits.

Serves 4-6

225g/8 oz cooked meat, such as beef, ham or chicken
85g/3 oz butter, softened, plus extra for melting
½ tsp freshly grated nutmeg
salt and freshly ground black pepper
dash of Worcestershire sauce (optional)

1. Put the meat in a processor and buzz until finely chopped. Alternatively, mince it finely.

2. Add the meat to the butter and nutmeg and beat until smooth. Season to taste with salt, pepper and Worcestershire sauce (optional).

3. Spoon into one large dish, or several small ones. Melt a little extra butter and pour a thin layer on top of each dish, sufficient to just cover the meat mixture.

4. Cover and chill for at least 2 hours.

Potted Salmon

Potted fish has always been popular in the North of England. Original recipes probably would have contained fish which had been cooked specifically for the dish. These days, it's a great recipe for using up leftover poached salmon or other fish. I like to keep the fish in flakes but, if you prefer a smooth mixture, give the fish a quick buzz in the processor. Lancashire and Yorkshire are famous for their shrimp teas – to make Potted Shrimps, use cooked, shelled shrimps in place of salmon and add a couple of pinches of freshly grated nutmeg. Serve it with slices of crisp toast.

Serves 4-6

225g/8 oz cooked salmon, weighed after removal of skin and bones
85g/3 oz butter, softened
salt and freshly ground pepper
2 tbsp chopped fresh herbs, such as dill, parsley or chives
extra butter for melting (optional)

1. Put the fish into a bowl with the butter, season with salt and pepper and add the herbs. Mix until well combined.

2. Spoon into one large dish, or several small ones. If you wish, melt some extra butter and pour a thin layer on top of each dish, sufficient to just cover the salmon mixture.

3. Cover and chill for at least 2 hours.

Cauliflower Cheese

Cauliflower is known to have been eaten by the Ancient Greeks and Romans. This simple dish dates as far back as the 17th century. It was certainly a favourite with my children when they were small. Make it in one large dish or in individual serving dishes. For a change, try adding some wholegrain mustard or a few dashes of Worcestershire sauce to the cooked cheese sauce. Alternatively, vary the type of cheese you use – I have used Cheddar but try adding crumbled blue cheese or your own favourite (well-flavoured) variety. Serve it with a green salad and some crusty bread.

Serves 4

1 medium cauliflower, trimmed and cut into florets
25g/1 oz butter
25g/1 oz plain flour
300ml/½ pt milk
85-115g/3-4 oz mature Cheddar cheese, grated
salt and freshly ground pepper

1. Cook the cauliflower in salted boiling water for 5-8 minutes or until just tender. Drain well and tip into one large or four small flameproof dish(es).

2. Meanwhile, melt the butter in a saucepan and stir in the flour. Cook gently for 1-2 minutes without allowing it to brown. Remove from the heat and gradually stir in the milk. Cook, stirring, until the sauce comes to the boil and thickens. Simmer very gently for a further 2 minutes, stirring. Add half the cheese and season to taste.

3. Pour the sauce over the hot cauliflower and sprinkle with the remaining cheese.

4. Put under a hot grill for a couple of minutes until bubbling and golden brown.

To microwave:

1. Put the cauliflower into a casserole with 4 tbsp water, cover and cook on HIGH for about 5 minutes, stirring once, until just tender. Drain well and tip into one large or four small flameproof dish(es).

2. Put the butter in a bowl or jug and cook on HIGH for about 20 seconds until melted. Stir in the flour and cook on HIGH for 20 seconds. Gradually stir in the milk, then cook on HIGH for about 3 minutes, stirring frequently, or until the sauce comes to the boil and thickens. Add half the cheese and season to taste.

3. Pour the sauce over the hot cauliflower and sprinkle with the remaining cheese.

4. Put under a hot grill for a couple of minutes until bubbling and golden brown.

Scotch Eggs

This method of wrapping sausagemeat around whole eggs was developed in Scotland, where they were served for breakfast. Usually served cold, they make ideal finger food for picnics and, cut into quarters and served with a variety of salads, great party food for hungry teenagers. For the best flavour, buy some of your favourite meaty sausages and remove their skins. To the sausagemeat, I like to add a good dash of Worcestershire or chilli sauce, or a few tablespoons of fresh chopped herbs, such as chives and thyme.

Makes 4

4 eggs
1 tbsp plain flour
salt and freshly ground black pepper
225g/8 oz sausagemeat
1 medium egg, beaten
fresh breadcrumbs
oil for deep-frying

1. To hard-boil the eggs, cover them with cold water, bring to the boil, then simmer gently for 10 minutes. Drain and cool under cold running water and, to prevent the yolk discolouring, lightly crack the shells. Leave until cold before removing the shells.

2. Season the flour with salt and pepper. Coat the shelled eggs with the flour mixture.

3. Divide the sausagemeat into four equal portions. Press one quarter into a flat cake and shape it evenly around the egg, sealing the joins well and making sure there are no cracks. Repeat with the remaining sausagemeat and eggs.

4. One at a time, coat the eggs in the beaten egg and then in the breadcrumbs.

5. Heat the oil in a deep fat fryer to 160°-180°C/325°-350°F. Gently lower the eggs into the oil and cook for about 8 minutes until the sausagemeat is brown and cooked all over. Lift out and drain on absorbent paper and leave to cool.

Toad in the Hole

There are many theories about how this dish, and its name, came into being. One thing is for certain, it has been a popular, economical dish across Britain for many a year. It is delicious served with fried onions and gravy.

Serves 4

2 tbsp oil
450g/1 lb meaty sausages
115g/4 oz plain flour
pinch of salt
150ml/¼ pt milk
1 medium egg

1. Put the oil in a small roasting tin and add the sausages. Cook at 220°C/425°F/Gas 7 for about 10 minutes until the fat is very hot and the sausages are beginning to brown.

2. Meanwhile, sift the flour and salt into a bowl. Mix the milk with 150ml/¼ pt water. Break the egg into the flour and gradually mix in the milk mixture, beating well to make a smooth batter.

3. Lift the roasting tin out of the oven, quickly pour in the batter and return it to the hot oven.

4. Continue cooking for about 45 minutes until the batter is puffed up and golden brown.

Corned Beef Hash

This recipe was particularly popular in the 1940s, when wartime greatly reduced the availability of foods, and canned and home-grown produce came to the fore. Corned Beef Hash is a delicious way of using up leftover potatoes. Pep it up with the addition of Worcestershire sauce or Chilli sauce. Sometimes I add tomatoes (skinned and quartered) or thin slices of red or yellow pepper at the beginning of step 2. Waxy potatoes are best, like British-grown Cara, Estima or Wilja.

Serves 4

2 tbsp oil
25g/1 oz butter
1 large onion, thinly sliced
550g/1¼ lb cooked potatoes, cut into small cubes
300g can corned beef, cut into small cubes
salt and freshly ground black pepper
2 tbsp chopped fresh parsley

1. Heat the oil and butter in a frying pan and add the onion. Cook gently for 5-10 minutes, stirring frequently, until soft but not brown.

2. Stir in the potatoes and corned beef. Season with salt and pepper. Cook over medium heat for about 15 minutes, stirring occasionally, or until the mixture is full of crispy brown patches.

3. Scatter the parsley over and serve immediately.

Sausage Rolls

Sausage rolls make ideal finger food for parties and picnics. You can of course buy sausage rolls already prepared and cooked, but they are unlikely to compare with the home-made version. For sausagemeat, buy your favourite meaty sausages from the butcher and simply remove their skins. To plain pork sausagemeat, add a couple of finely chopped spring onions and 1 tsp dried or fresh herbs. I like to use puff pastry, but shortcrust is just as good – the recipe uses ready-made but you can, of course, make your own. Serve hot or cooled, just as they are or with pickle and a salad garnish.

Makes about 12

350g/12 oz puff pastry, thawed if frozen
350g/12 oz sausagemeat
beaten egg

1. On a lightly floured surface, roll out the pastry into an oblong about 30cm/12 inches long. Cut lengthways into two long strips.
2. On a lightly floured surface, shape half the sausagemeat into a long roll, the same length as the pastry. Repeat with the remaining sausagemeat.
3. Lay a roll of meat on each pastry strip. Brush the pastry edges lightly with water. Fold the pastry over, pressing the edges together to seal it well. Turn the rolls over, seam side down.
4. Brush with beaten egg and cut each roll into six. With a sharp knife, make two or three shallow cuts in the top pastry of each one. Place on a baking tray.
5. Put into a preheated oven and cook at 220°C/425°F/Gas 7 for 20-25 minutes until golden brown and cooked through.

Herrings in Oatmeal

This traditional Scottish dish is so simple and, in my opinion, is one of the best ways to serve herrings. Ask your fishmonger to remove heads and bones. Alternatively, buy ready-boned herrings. I like to fry them in oil and butter, though they are even more delicious when cooked in bacon fat. If you prefer not to use any extra fat (herrings are oily fish), they can be popped under a medium-hot grill, turning once until just cooked and flaky. Serve them with buttered slices of brown bread.

Serves 2

2 herrings, each weighing 175-225g/6-8 oz
salt and freshly ground pepper
55g/2 oz fine or medium oatmeal
1 tbsp oil
15g/½ oz butter
lemon wedges, to serve

1. Season the herrings, inside and out, with salt and pepper. Coat with the oatmeal, pressing it well into the fish.

2. Heat the oil and butter in a large frying pan and add the herrings. Cook over medium heat for about 5 minutes on each side, or until tender and golden.

3. Serve hot with lemon wedges for squeezing over.

Bubble and Squeak

This dish is named, seemingly, after the sounds it makes during cooking in the pan. Originally, it would have contained cooked beef too, then it developed into the classic way of turning leftover vegetables (and sometimes meat) into a tasty dish. It was particularly popular in London and the South East. I recall that, when I was a child in Wales, my mother used beef dripping for frying and she would add cooked sprouts as well as cabbage. These days, I like to cook Bubble and Squeak in a non-stick pan and serve it with a dash of hot chilli sauce or with a poached egg and a little crisp-cooked bacon.

Serves 2-4

1 tbsp olive oil
1 medium onion, thinly sliced
25g/1 oz butter
450g/1 lb cooked mashed potatoes
225g/8 oz cooked cabbage, roughly chopped
salt and freshly ground black pepper

1. Heat the oil in a frying pan and add the onion. Cook for about 5 minutes, stirring frequently, until soft but not brown.

2. Add the butter and stir until melted. Add the potatoes, cabbage and seasoning. Cook over medium heat until the underside is crisp and golden.

3. Turn it over (depending on the size of the pan, you may need to divide it into quarters first) and continue cooking until the second side is crisp and golden.

Macaroni Cheese

Macaroni became popular in this country in the 18th century. In the days of Queen Victoria, it was served at many supper tables. It's still one of my favourite standbys, served with a crunchy salad alongside it. Ring the changes by adding some cooked vegetables to the mixture before grilling – such as crisp broccoli florets, courgette slices or red pepper strips.

Serves 4

225g/8 oz macaroni
55g/2 oz butter
55g/2 oz plain flour
850ml/1½ pt milk
1 tbsp wholegrain or Dijon mustard
225g/8 oz mature Cheddar cheese, grated
salt and freshly ground pepper
2 tbsp fresh breadcrumbs

1. Cook the macaroni in plenty of boiling salted water, following the packet instructions, until tender.

2. Meanwhile, melt the butter in a saucepan and stir in the flour. Cook gently for 1-2 minutes without allowing it to brown. Remove from the heat and gradually stir in the milk. Cook, stirring, until the sauce comes to the boil and thickens. Simmer gently for a further 2 minutes, stirring. Add the mustard and three-quarters of the cheese. Season to taste.

3. Drain the macaroni well and stir into the sauce. Tip the mixture into one large or four small flameproof dish(es) and sprinkle the remaining cheese and the breadcrumbs over the top.

4. Put under a hot grill until bubbling and golden brown.

To microwave:

1. Put the macaroni into a large casserole and pour over sufficient boiling water (from the kettle) to cover it by about 2.5cm/1 in. Stir well. Cook, uncovered, on HIGH for about 10 minutes, stirring once or twice, or until just tender. Cover and leave to stand.

2. Meanwhile, put the butter in a bowl or jug and cook on HIGH for about 30 seconds until melted. Stir in the flour and cook on HIGH for 30 seconds. Gradually stir in the milk, then cook on HIGH for about 6 minutes, stirring frequently, or until the sauce comes to the boil and thickens. Add the mustard and three-quarters of the cheese. Season to taste.

3. Drain the macaroni well and stir into the sauce. Tip the mixture into one large or four small flameproof dish(es) and sprinkle the remaining cheese and the breadcrumbs over the top.

4. Put under a hot grill until bubbling and golden brown.

Glamorgan Sausages

In Wales, when times were hard, these provided an economical and tasty substitute for meat sausages. They would be served with mashed potatoes or chips. Today they have become a rather trendy dish on many restaurant menus, served with light salads and fruity sauces. The original mixture would have contained dried herbs, mustard powder and finely chopped onion or leek – I use fresh herbs, wholegrain mustard and thinly sliced leek.

Makes 8

150g/5½ oz fresh breadcrumbs, plus extra for coating
85g/3 oz grated mature Cheddar or Caerphilly cheese
1 small leek, thinly sliced
1-2 tbsp chopped fresh herbs, such as parsley, thyme and a very
  little sage
salt and freshly ground black pepper
2 medium eggs
1 tbsp wholegrain mustard
milk to mix, if necessary
about 2 tbsp plain flour
oil for deep-frying

1. Combine the breadcrumbs, cheese, leek and herbs. Season with salt and pepper. Lightly beat 1 whole egg with 1 egg yolk and the mustard. Stir into the breadcrumb mixture, adding sufficient milk to bind the mixture together if necessary.

2. Divide the mixture and shape into 8 sausages.

3. Lightly beat the remaining egg white. Coat each sausage in flour, then beaten egg white and then breadcrumbs. Cover and chill for 1 hour or until needed.

4. Heat the oil in a deep fat fryer to 180°C/350°F. Gently lower the sausages into the oil and cook for about 5 minutes until golden brown all over. Alternatively, fry in shallow oil in a frying pan, turning occasionally until golden brown all over.

5. Lift out, drain on kitchen paper and serve immediately.

Pan Haggerty

This dish is traditional in the north of England and, particularly, in Northumberland. Panhaggerty (one word) means 'onions and potatoes'. Like many of our potato-based recipes, I guess this one was created to provide a substantial and well-flavoured meal which was also economical. Use firm textured British-grown potatoes such as Cara, Desirée, Maris Piper, Romano or Wilja. A heavy-bottomed frying pan works best. Serve it, straight from the pan, just as it is or with roast or grilled meat.

Serves 4

25g/1 oz butter
1 tbsp oil
450g/1 lb potatoes, peeled and thinly sliced
225g/8 oz onions, thinly sliced
115g/4 oz grated cheese (Cheddar or Lancashire are good)
salt and freshly ground black pepper

1. Put the butter and oil in a frying pan and heat until melted. Swirl it around the base of the pan.

2. Add layers of potatoes, onions and cheese, seasoning between each layer and finishing with a layer of cheese.

3. Cover and cook over a gentle heat for about 30 minutes, or until the vegetables are tender (test them with the point of a sharp knife) and the underside is brown.

4. Uncover and brown the top under a hot grill. Alternatively, turn the potato (invert the 'cake' on to a flat plat, then carefully slide it back into the pan) and cook over medium heat until the underside is brown.

Clapshot

This delicious way of serving mashed potato is traditional in
Scotland, where Clapshot is often served with haggis. Use the
orange-fleshed root vegetable that the Scots call turnip and is
known as swede in the South with British-grown floury potatoes, such as King Edward or Desirée. It is often served with
crispy bits of grilled bacon scattered over the top. Using
chopped spring onions in place of the chives and extra potatoes
in place of the turnip produces the Irish dish called Champ.

Serves 4

450g/1 lb floury potatoes, peeled and cut into chunks
450g/1 lb turnip (swede – see note), peeled and cut into thin
  chunks
salt and freshly ground black pepper
150ml/¼ pt milk
55g/2 oz butter
3 tbsp snipped fresh chives

1. Put the potatoes and turnip (swede) in a pan and bring to the boil
   in lightly salted water. Cover and cook gently for about 20
   minutes or until tender.

2. Drain and return the vegetables to the pan. Mash until smooth.

3. Beat in the milk and butter. Season to taste and stir in the chives.

To microwave:
1. Put the potatoes and turnip (swede) into a large casserole with
   4 tbsp water. Cover and cook on HIGH for about 12 minutes,
   stirring occasionally, or until tender.

2. Drain and return the vegetables to the casserole. Mash until
   smooth.

3. Beat in the milk and butter. Season to taste and stir in the chives.

Punchnep

In this dish, of Welsh origin, the mashed potatoes are given an almost translucent quality with the addition of an equal quantity of white turnips. Use British-grown floury potatoes, such as King Edward or Desirée. Serve each person with a mound of potato, make a well in the centre and pour in some cream. I like to serve it with some freshly cooked slices of leek.

Serves 4

450g/1 lb floury potatoes, peeled and cut into chunks
450g/1 lb turnips, peeled and cut into chunks
115g/4 oz butter
salt and freshly ground black pepper
4 tbsp cream (double, single, soured or crème fraîche)

1. Put the potatoes and turnips in a pan and bring to the boil in lightly salted water. Cover and cook gently for about 20 minutes or until tender.

2. Drain and return the vegetables to the pan. Add the butter and mash until smooth. Season to taste.

3. Serve in mounds, make a well in the centre of each and spoon in some cream.

To microwave:
1. Put the potatoes and turnips into a large casserole with 4 tbsp water. Cover and cook on HIGH for about 12 minutes, stirring occasionally, or until tender.

2. Drain and return the vegetables to the casserole. Add the butter and mash until smooth. Season to taste.

3. Serve in mounds, make a well in the centre of each and spoon in some cream.

Stump

A typically Northern dish, this winter dish is a purée of root vegetables – potatoes, swede (called turnip in Scotland) and carrots. Vary the quantities (and colour) to suit yourself, but do use British-grown floury potatoes, such as King Edward or Desirée.

Serves 4

225g/8 oz floury potatoes, peeled and cut into chunks
225g/8 oz swede, peeled and cut into thin chunks
225g/8 oz carrots, peeled and thinly sliced
salt and freshly ground black pepper
150ml/¼ pt milk
25g/1 oz butter

1. Put the three vegetables in a pan and bring to the boil in lightly salted water. Cover and cook gently for about 20 minutes or until tender.
2. Drain and return the vegetables to the pan. Add the milk and butter and mash until smooth, seasoning to taste.

To microwave:
1. Put the vegetables into a large casserole with 4 tbsp water. Cover and cook on HIGH for 10-12 minutes, stirring occasionally, or until tender.
2. Drain and return the vegetables to the casserole. Add the milk and butter and mash until smooth, seasoning to taste.

Cheese Pudding

Cheese Pudding is one of those traditional dishes that seems to have been passed over for more exotic things. Still, it remains one of my favourite recipes using ingredients which are usually at hand. The original version would have used mustard powder – today we have a wide variety of ready-made mustards which can be used instead.

Serves 4

225g/8 oz grated British cheese, such as Cheddar
115g/4 oz fresh breadcrumbs
600ml/1 pt milk
40g/1½ oz butter
3 medium eggs, beaten
1 tsp mustard, such as English or wholegrain
salt and freshly ground black pepper

1. Butter a 1.2 litre/2 pt soufflé dish.

2. Combine three-quarters of the cheese with the breadcrumbs.

3. Put the remaining ingredients into a pan and mix well. Heat gently, stirring, until the butter has just melted (the mixture must not be too hot).

4. Pour over the cheese mixture and stir gently. Tip into the prepared dish and scatter the remaining cheese over the top.

5. Put into a preheated oven and cook at 200°C/400°F/Gas 6 for about 30 minutes or until set and golden. The pudding is cooked when a knife inserted in the centre comes out clean.

To microwave:

1. Follow steps 1 and 2 above.

2. Put the remaining ingredients into a bowl and mix well. Cook on HIGH for 1-2 minutes, stirring once or twice, until the butter has just melted (the mixture must not be too hot).

3. Follow step 4 above.

4. Cook on MED-LOW for about 15 minutes or until set. The pudding is cooked when a knife inserted in the centre comes out clean.

5. If wished, lightly brown the top of the pudding under a hot grill.

Pease Pudding

'Pease Pudding hot,
Pease Pudding cold,
Pease Pudding in the pot,
Nine days old.
Some like it hot,
Some like it cold,
Some like it in the pot
Nine days old.'

The nursery rhyme says it all!

A traditional English accompaniment to boiled bacon, the peas would, originally, have been cooked with a ham bone for flavour. In the recipe below, I have added a ham stock cube, but you could just as easily add some finely chopped lean bacon. Any leftover Pease Pudding can be frozen, ready for reheating at a later date.

Serves 6

450g/1 lb split dried peas, soaked overnight in plenty of cold water
1 ham stock cube
25g/1 oz butter
1 egg
salt and freshly ground pepper

1. Drain the peas and put into a large saucepan. Pour over boiling water to cover generously. Add the stock cube and stir until dissolved. Bring to the boil over a gentle heat, then boil rapidly for 10 minutes.

2. Cover the pan and simmer gently for about 2 hours, stirring occasionally and adding small amounts of boiling water if the peas become too dry, until the peas are soft.

3. Drain off excess water, then either tip the peas into a processor and purée until smooth or push them through a sieve.

4. Add the butter and egg and mix well. Season to taste with salt and pepper.

5. Spoon the mixture into a 20cm/8 in buttered ovenproof dish and cook at 180°C/350°F/Gas 4 for about 30 minutes, until set.

To microwave:

1. Drain the peas and put into a large casserole. Pour over boiling water to cover generously. Add the stock cube and stir until dissolved. Cook on HIGH until the mixture comes to the boil, then boil rapidly on HIGH for 10 minutes.

2. Cover and cook on MED-LOW for about 1 hour, stirring occasionally, or until the peas are very soft.

3. Drain off excess water, then either tip the peas into a processor and purée until smooth or push them through a sieve.

4. Add the butter and egg and mix well. Season to taste with salt and pepper.

5. Spoon the mixture into a buttered 20cm/8 in soufflé dish. Cook on MED-LOW for about 10 minutes until set.

Welsh Rarebit

The Welsh name for this dish is *Caws Pobi* or grilled cheese. Years ago it was customary to lay a slice of cold roast beef and some mustard or horseradish on the toast before pouring the melted cheese over. The recipe below is delicious but I think it tastes even better when beer is used (brown ale is best) in place of milk. When time is really short, I just mix all the ingredients together, add a beaten egg and spread the mixture thickly on the toast before grilling. For a spicier dish, add extra mustard, some Worcestershire sauce, curry paste or a little cayenne pepper. It's also good with some chopped fresh herbs stirred into the melting cheese. For Buck Rarebit, prepare the recipe as below and top each piece of cheesy toast with a poached egg.

Serves 4

225g/8 oz Cheddar cheese, grated
25g/1 oz butter
4 tbsp milk
1 tsp mustard powder
salt and freshly ground black pepper
4 thick slices of hot toast

1. Put the cheese into a saucepan and add the butter, milk, mustard powder and seasoning. Heat very gently, stirring occasionally, until the cheese has melted and the mixture is smooth and creamy.

2. Pour the cheese mixture over the toast and put under a hot grill until bubbling and golden brown.

3. Serve immediately.

Colcannon

Irish in origin, Colcannon was traditionally eaten at Halloween with charms added to the potato mixture – a ring, button, coin, thimble and horseshoe. Whoever was served the ring could expect to marry within the year.

Use British-grown floury potatoes, such as King Edward or Desirée. If you prefer, leave out the onions and flavour the potatoes with some freshly grated nutmeg.

Serves 4

550g/1¼ lb floury potatoes, peeled and cut into chunks
salt and freshly ground black pepper
225g/8 oz green cabbage, finely shredded
3 spring onions, thinly sliced
55g/2 oz butter

1. Put the potatoes in a pan and bring to the boil in lightly salted water. Cover and cook gently for about 20 minutes or until tender.

2. Drain well and return the potatoes to the pan. Mash until smooth, then season to taste.

3. Put the cabbage and onions into a pan with about 3 tbsp water. Cover and cook over a low heat for about 3 minutes until soft.

4. Gently stir the cabbage mixture into the potatoes. Spoon into a buttered flameproof dish, large enough to hold a depth of about 5cm/2 in. Push knobs of butter into the surface.

5. Cook in a preheated oven at 200°/400°/Gas 6 for about 25 minutes or until crisp and golden.

To microwave:

1. Put the potatoes into a large casserole with 4 tbsp water. Cover and cook on HIGH for about 10 minutes, stirring occasionally, until tender.

2. Follow step 2 above.

3. Put the cabbage and onions into a casserole with 2 tbsp water. Cover and cook on HIGH for about 4 minutes, stirring once, until just soft.

4. Follow step 4 above.

5. Cook on MED-HIGH for about 2 minutes or until the mixture is hot and the butter has melted. Brown under a hot grill if wished.

Fish Cakes

Fish cakes have recently come back into fashion and are served, in their various forms, in many restaurants. In place of the heavy, tasteless cakes that some of us remember from our school days, we now have light delicious concoctions, crisp on the outside and meltingly soft on the inside and made with a variety of fish. Fish cakes are best made with equal quantities of fish and mashed potato. You can of course use leftover mashed potatoes, but the result is far better if they are freshly prepared and mashed. Serve them piping hot with a green salad tossed in vinegar-and-oil dressing.

Serves 4

450g/1 lb skinless fish fillets, such as plain or smoked haddock or
    cod, salmon, or a mixture
450g/1 lb cooked mashed potato
55g/2 oz butter, melted
2 tbsp chopped fresh parsley or dill
1 lemon
salt and freshly ground black pepper
beaten egg
115g/4 oz breadcrumbs (made from stale bread)
oil for frying

1. Put the fish into a shallow pan and add about 300ml/½ pt water. Heat gently until the water just comes to the boil. Cover and cook very gently for 8-10 minutes or until the fish is just cooked. Using a slotted spoon, transfer the fish to a plate. Flake the flesh, removing any bones.

2. Put the potato into a large bowl and add the fish, butter and herb. Finely grate the rind from ½ the lemon and add to the bowl. Cut the remaining lemon half into wedges and reserve. Season the fish mixture with salt and plenty of pepper. Using your hand, gently mix the ingredients together and shape into eight cakes. (At this point, they can be refrigerated for 30 minutes-2 hours, after which they will be easier to handle.)

3. Brush the cakes with beaten egg and coat them in the bread-crumbs.

4. Heat some oil in a large frying pan and cook the fish cakes over medium heat for 5-10 minutes on each side, until crisp and golden brown.

5. Serve with the reserved lemon wedges for squeezing over.

To microwave:
1. Put the fish into a dish, large enough to hold it in one layer. Add 150ml/¼ pt water. Cover and cook on HIGH for about 4 minutes or until the fish is just cooked.

2. Put the potato into a large bowl and add the fish, butter and herb. Finely grat the rind from ½ the lemon and add to the bowl. Cut the remaining lemon half into wedges and reserve. Season the fish mixture with salt and plenty of pepper. Using your hand, gently mix the ingredients together and shape into eight cakes. (At this point, they can be refrigerated for 30 minutes-2 hours, after which they will be easier to handle.)

3. Brush the cakes with beaten egg and coat them in the breadcrumbs.

4. Heat some oil in a large frying pan and cook the fish cakes over medium heat for 5-10 minutes on each side, until crisp and golden brown.

5. Serve with the reserved lemon wedges for squeezing over.

Cornish Pasties

The Cornish Pasty or Tiddly Oggie can be traced back to the mid 19th century and, in years gone by, would have been made with many different fillings. Then, pasties provided the miners and labourers of Cornwall with a portable meal. The pastry was often marked on one end with an initial – so that the workers could recognise which half-eaten (huge) pasty belonged to whom. Folklore has it that the devil never crossed the Tamar from Devon into Cornwall in case he turned into a pasty! Here is just one version of the traditional beef, potato, and vegetable filling, wrapped up in a parcel of shortcrust pastry. The smaller you cut the steak and vegetables, the better the flavour will be. Serve the pasties warm or cold.

Makes 4

450g/1 lb lean rump steak, fat trimmed off, finely chopped
225g/8 oz potatoes, finely chopped
225g/8 oz swede, finely chopped
1 medium onion, finely chopped
2 tbsp chopped fresh parsley
salt and freshly ground black pepper
450g/1 lb shortcrust pastry
25g/1 oz butter
beaten egg

1. In a large bowl, mix together the steak, vegetables and parsley, seasoning generously with salt and pepper.

2. On a lightly floured surface, roll out the pastry and cut out four 20cm/8 in circles.

3. Spoon the filling into the centre of each pastry circle and top each with a knob of butter. Brush the pastry edges with a little water, then fold the pastry over the filling into a half-moon shape. Seal and crimp the edges.

4. Arrange the pasties on a greased baking sheet and brush with beaten egg.

5. Cook in a preheated oven at 220°C/425°F/Gas 7 for 10 minutes then continue cooking at 180°C/350°C/Gas 4 for a further ¾-1 hour.

Stovies

A Scottish potato dish which typically was served on a Monday, following the Sunday roast. If you want to be really traditional, replace the water with gravy and the butter with dripping from the roast. Add some chopped pieces of cooked chicken or meat too if you like (at the end of step 2). Cook the potatoes very gently (particularly if gravy is added) to prevent them sticking to the bottom of the pan. Serve them hot, straight from the pan.

Serves 4

25g/1 oz butter
1 large onion, very thinly sliced
450g/1 lb potatoes, thickly sliced or halved if small
salt and freshly ground black pepper

1. Melt the butter in a heavy-base frying pan. Add the onion and cook gently for about 5 minutes, stirring occasionally, until it begins to soften.

2. Add the potatoes to the pan and turn them over, making sure they are all coated with the hot butter. Season with salt and pepper. Gently press the mixture down to make an even layer. Pour over 150ml/¼ pt water. Cover with a circle of greaseproof paper and then a lid (this helps to keep as much moisture as possible in the pan to prevent the mixture from sticking).

3. Cook very gently for about 30 minutes, shaking the pan occasionally with the lid on, until the potatoes are cooked through and crisp and brown on the bottom.

3

MAIN MEALS

This is the place to find all those substantial main-meal dishes that reflect our British heritage. No matter which part of the British Isles you come from, there is something to remind you of home and of food in 'the old days'.

Lamb with Honey and Herbs

Welsh lamb enjoys international recognition for its leanness, succulence and taste. It's delicious when roasted and served with freshly-made mint sauce. In the recipe below, honey and herbs give sweetness and aromatic flavour to this traditional way of cooking shoulder of lamb (the sweetest meat) in Wales. If you like garlic, use extra, cut it into slivers and insert them into slits in the lamb (made with the tip of a sharp knife). I like it served simply with new potatoes and buttered carrots.

Serves 6

1.35kg/3 lb shoulder of lamb
1 plump garlic clove, halved
salt and freshly ground black pepper
5 tbsp clear honey
300ml/½ pt dry cider, plus extra if necessary
1 tsp chopped fresh rosemary
1 tsp chopped fresh mint
1 tsp chopped fresh thyme
1 tsp fresh lemon juice

1. Rub the lamb all over with the cut sides of the garlic. Put the joint in a roasting tin and season with salt and pepper.

2. Stir the honey into the cider and add the herbs. Pour over the lamb and cover with foil.

3. Cook in a preheated oven at 220°C/425°F/Gas 7 for 30 minutes.

4. Lift the foil and baste (spoon the juices over) the lamb. Replace the foil and continue cooking at 180°C/350°F/Gas 4 for about 1 hour, basting occasionally and adding a little extra cider if necessary, until the lamb is tender. Remove the foil for the final 20-30 minutes cooking.

5. Lift the lamb on to a serving plate and leave to 'relax' for 10 minutes before carving. Spoon any excess fat off the top of the juices in the tin, stir in the lemon juice and serve with the lamb.

Roast Beef with Yorkshire Pudding and Gravy

This Yorkshire combination has become traditional all over the British Isles. When most of us think of roast beef and Yorkshire pudding, we automatically think of Sunday lunch. In Yorkshire, the batter pudding would have been (and often still is) served with the gravy before the meat course – in leaner times it was hoped that you would then eat less meat.

For the beef joint, choose rib, sirloin, rump or topside, allowing about 175-225g/6-8 oz per person. Allow the meat to come to room temperature before cooking. Once the meat is cooked, it is removed from the oven and left to 'relax' while you cook the Yorkshire puddings.

My family likes plenty of thickened gravy but, if you prefer, the meat juices can be used just as they are (after the excess fat is poured off) or boiled up with beef stock, red wine or, if you are boiling vegetables to accompany the dish, some of their cooking liquor. When the beef is carved, the juices which run from it can be stirred into the gravy too. If you like a really dark gravy, add some gravy browning (a flavourless natural colouring).

Serves 6

joint of beef weighing about 1.35kg/3 lb (see note above)
25g/1 oz beef dripping or 2 tbsp oil
1 tsp mustard powder (optional)
freshly ground black pepper

Yorkshire Puddings:
55g/2 oz plain flour
pinch of salt
1 small or medium egg
75ml/2½ fl oz milk

Gravy:
1-2 tbsp plain flour
about 300ml/½ pt beef stock or vegetable cooking liquor (see note above)

1. Put the beef on a rack in a shallow roasting tin, fat side up. Rub the joint all over with the dripping or oil, mustard powder (optional) and pepper.

2. Cook in a preheated oven at 180°C/350°F/Gas 4 for: *rare* – about 1 hour 20 minutes (20 minutes per 450g/1 lb plus an extra 20 minutes); *medium done* – about 1 hour 40 minutes (25 minutes per 450g/1 lb plus an extra 25 minutes); *well done* – about 2 hours (30 minutes per 450g/1 lb plus an extra 30 minutes). Baste (spoon the fat and juices over) the beef several times during cooking.

3. Meanwhile, make the batter for the Yorkshire Puddings. Sift the flour and salt into a large bowl or jug. Make a well in the centre and break the egg into it. Add about half the milk and, using a wooden spoon, gradually blend in the flour to make a smooth mixture. Add the remaining milk and 75ml/2½ fl oz cold water and beat well. Leave to stand until needed.

4. At the end of its cooking time, remove the beef from the oven, transfer it to a warmed plate, cover with foil and leave to stand for about 15 minutes.

5. Meanwhile, increase the oven temperature to 220°C/425°F/Gas 7. Put ½ tsp fat from the roasting tin into each of 12 patty tins. Put into the oven until very hot and the fat begins to haze. Quickly pour an equal quantity of the pudding batter into each tin and return the tray to the oven. Cook at 220°C/425°F/Gas 7 for about 15 minutes until well risen and golden brown (do not open the oven door during cooking).

6. To make the gravy, pour off the excess fat from the roasting tin, leaving the sediment and about 1 tbsp fat behind. Stir in the flour and cook gently, stirring continuously and scraping all the brown sediment from the bottom of the tin, until brown. Remove from the heat and gradually stir in the stock. Cook, stirring, until the gravy comes to the boil and thickens, then simmer gently for 2-3 minutes. Adjust the seasoning if necessary.

7. Serve the beef, sliced, with the gravy and Yorkshire Puddings.

Crown Roast of Lamb

In Edwardian days, this was considered to be a most elegant dish. More recently, it has graced many a dinner-party table, with the tips of the 'crown' decorated with paper frills. A similarly 'royal' dish is Guard of Honour, in which two trimmed best ends of neck are positioned, fat side facing out, to form an arch with their bones interlaced and the stuffing in the centre. Your butcher will be happy to prepare the lamb for you, but do remember to order it in advance. Serve it with a variety of seasonal vegetables.

Serves 6

2 best end necks of lamb (6 cutlets in each), chined (backbone removed)

Stuffing:
25g/1 oz butter
1 medium onion, finely chopped
2 celery sticks, thinly sliced
10 ready-to-eat dried apricots, finely chopped
115g/4 oz fresh breadcrumbs
2 tbsp finely chopped fresh mint
finely grated rind and juice of 1 lemon
1 medium egg, beaten
salt and freshly ground black pepper

Gravy:
2 tbsp plain flour
425ml/¾ pt lamb or vegetable stock

1. In a saucepan, melt the butter and add the onion and celery. Cook over medium heat for about 5 minutes, stirring occasionally, until soft but not brown. Remove from the heat and stir in the remaining stuffing ingredients. Leave to cool.

2. Meanwhile, trim and scrape the meat off the top 2.5cm/1 in of each bone. Curve the joints, with the fat side in, to make a circle or 'crown'. Using fine string, sew the ends together. Wrap small pieces of foil around the trimmed ends of the bones.

3. Spoon the stuffing into the centre of the lamb. Weigh the stuffed joint, then put into a roasting tin.

4. Cook in a preheated oven at 180°C/350°C/Gas 4 for 25 minutes per 450g/1 lb plus an extra 25 minutes. Baste (spoon fat and juices over) occasionally during cooking.

5. Transfer the lamb to a serving dish and keep warm.

6. Drain the fat from the tin, leaving the sediment and 2 tbsp fat behind. Mix in the flour and cook over low heat, stirring, for about 2 minutes. Remove from the heat and gradually stir in the stock. Cook over medium heat, stirring, until the gravy comes to the boil and thickens slightly. Continue cooking gently for 2-3 minutes. Season to taste.

7. Carve the lamb into cutlets and serve with the stuffing and gravy.

Shepherd's Pie

Often called Cottage Pie, depending on which part of the British Isles you come from, this dish is now a countrywide favourite. Traditionally, it is made with lamb or beef. Its flavour can be bland or highly seasoned and it can be made with raw or cooked meat. I prefer to use raw meat but if you have some left over from a cooked joint, mince or chop it finely and add it to the softened vegetables in step 2 (use only 1 tbsp flour and 150ml/¼ pt stock and simmer for just a few minutes). Sometimes, I add a crushed garlic clove or two with the onion and a tablespoon of Worcestershire sauce with the stock. To add extra flavour and colour, sprinkle some finely grated mature cheese over the top of the potatoes before putting into the oven.

Serves 4

900g/2 lb British floury potatoes, such as King Edward or Desirée
salt and freshly ground black pepper
4 tbsp milk
25g/1 oz butter
1 tbsp oil
1 large onion, finely chopped
1 medium carrot, finely chopped
450g/1 lb lean minced lamb or beef
2 tbsp flour
300ml/½ pt lamb or beef stock
1 tbsp tomato purée
2 tsp dried mixed herbs

1. Cook the potatoes in boiling salted water for about 20 minutes or until tender. Drain and mash with the milk and butter, seasoning to taste with salt and pepper.

2. Heat the oil in a frying pan, add the onion and carrot and cook for 5-10 minutes, stirring occasionally, until soft. Add the meat and cook for about 5 minutes, stirring to separate it, until brown. Stir in the flour, then gradually stir in the stock. Add the tomato purée and herbs. Cook, stirring, until the mixture comes to the boil and thickens. Continue to simmer gently for about 30 minutes. Season to taste.

3. Tip the meat mixture into an ovenproof dish and spoon the mashed potato over the top.

4. Cook in a preheated oven at 190°C/375°F/Gas 5 for about 30 minutes until the potatoes are crisp and golden.

To microwave:

1. Cut the potatoes into cubes and put into a large casserole with 4 tbsp water. Cover and cook on HIGH for about 12 minutes, stirring once or twice, or until tender. Drain and mash with the milk and butter, seasoning to taste with salt and pepper.

2. Put the oil, onion and carrot into a casserole, cover and cook on HIGH for 5 minutes, stirring once, until soft. Stir in the meat, cover and cook for 5 minutes, stirring once. Stir in the flour, then the stock. Add the tomato purée and herbs. Cover and cook on HIGH for about 15 minutes, stirring occasionally, until the meat is tender. Season to taste.

3. Tip the meat mixture into a flameproof dish and spoon the mashed potato over the top.

4. Cook on MEDIUM for 10-15 minutes or until hot throughout, then brown the top under a hot grill.

Steak and Kidney Pie

Surprisingly, it seems that Steak and Kidney Pie dates back only to the early part of the 20th century, though beef pies would have been served as far back as Medieval times. As well as beef and kidney, it contained oysters (which were "poor man's food"). For authenticity, you could of course replace the mushrooms in the recipe below with oysters. For a change, try adding a tablespoon of Worcestershire sauce in step 3, or using brown ale in place of stock. The filling needs to be cooked slowly in order to develop the flavours. If time does not allow you to complete the whole dish at once, make the filling and freeze it at the end of step 4, then complete the pie on another day.

Serves 4

2 tbsp flour
salt and freshly ground black pepper
675g/1½ lb lean braising steak, cut into cubes
175g/6 oz ox kidney, trimmed and cut into small pieces
1 tbsp oil
15g/½ oz butter
1 medium onion chopped
1 garlic clove, crushed
300ml/½ pt beef stock
1 tbsp tomato purée
2 tsp dried mixed herbs
115g/4 oz closed cup mushrooms, thickly sliced
175-225g/6-8 oz puff pastry, thawed if frozen
beaten egg, to glaze

1. Season the flour with salt and pepper, then coat the steak and kidney pieces with it.

2. In a large saucepan, heat the oil and butter. Add the onion and garlic and cook over medium heat for about 5 minutes, stirring occasionally, until soft but not brown.

3. Add the steak and kidney and cook over high heat, stirring occasionally, until lightly browned. Stir in the stock, tomato purée and herbs. Heat, stirring, until the mixture just comes to the boil.

4. Cover and cook over a low heat, simmering gently, for about 1½ hours, stirring occasionally, or until the beef is tender (alternatively, cook in a preheated oven at 170°C/325°F/Gas 3 for a similar time).

5. Adjust the seasoning if necessary, stir in the mushrooms, then tip into a 1.7 litre/3 pt pie dish.

6. Roll out the pastry about 2.5cm/1 in larger than the dish. Cut off a 1cm/½ in strip from around the edge. Brush the rim of the dish with water and lay the strip on it. Lightly brush the strip with water, lay the pastry sheet on top and use a sharp knife to trim it to fit. Use the trimmings to decorate the top. Brush the pastry with beaten egg (over the top but not along the cut edges or they will not rise).

7. Cook in a preheated oven at 200°C/400°F/Gas 6 for about 45 minutes or until the pastry is puffed up and golden brown.

Irish Stew

Irish Stew is made with the same basic ingredients as Lancashire Hotpot – lamb, potatoes and onions. The original version would have been cooked over a peat fire, the lid having been sealed to the pot with a thick paste of flour and water to keep in the moisture and flavour. If you have time, give the dish extra flavour and colour by quickly browning the lamb in a little hot oil before adding it to the casserole (after browning, discard the excess oil, add the stock to the pan and stir in the sediment which will have stuck to the bottom – then pour into the casserole). The recipe below uses lean lamb. If you prefer to use cutlets, you will need about 675g/1½ lb.

Serves 4

450g/1 lb lean lamb, such as leg or fillet, cut into cubes
2 medium onions, thinly sliced
900g/2 lb potatoes, sliced
1 tsp dried herbs, such as thyme
salt and freshly ground black pepper
300ml/½ pt lamb or vegetable stock
freshly chopped parsley

1. Arrange alternate layers of lamb, onion and potato in a casserole, seasoning with the herbs, salt and pepper and finishing with a top layer of potato. Pour the stock over.

2. Cover and cook in a preheated oven at 180°C/375°F/Gas 4 for about 2½ hours.

3. Serve, sprinkled with parsley.

Boiled Beef and Carrots

"Boiled beef and carrots, boiled beef and carrots, she looks sweet . . ." goes the Cockney tune sung in old London music halls. Slow cooking makes this a meltingly tender dish. Serve it with a green vegetable and some creamy mashed potatoes.

Years ago, this meal would have been made with salted beef and, if you can get it (ask your local butcher), do use it. If the beef is very salty, you will need to soak it in plenty of cold water for several hours or overnight, then rinse it. As it cooks, the greyish colour of the salted beef will change to pink.

Serves 6

piece of lean silverside or brisket, weighing about1.6kg/3½ lb
2 tsp salt (do not use this with salted beef)
bouquet garni
6 black peppercorns
2 medium onions, sliced
2 celery sticks, thickly sliced
1 medium turnip, cut into wedges
1 medium leek, sliced
18-24 baby carrots

1. Put the beef into a large heavy-based saucepan and pour over sufficient water to just cover it. Heat slowly until it comes to the boil then, with a slotted spoon, skim the surface.

2. To the water, add the salt, bouquet garni, peppercorns and onions. Cover and simmer very gently for about 1½ hours.

3. Add the celery, turnip and leek, cover and simmer gently for 30 minutes.

4. Add the carrots, cover and simmer gently for a further 30 minutes or until the carrots are tender.

5. Lift out the beef and vegetables, discarding the bouquet garni, and arrange on a serving plate. Keep warm.

6. Heat the cooking liquid and boil quickly until slightly reduced, adjusting the seasoning if necessary. Serve with the beef (cut into slices) and the vegetables.

Boiled Bacon with Parsley Sauce

As a child, in Wales, this was one of my favourite treats. These days, I like to serve it with small new or tiny jacket potatoes. Use smoked or unsmoked bacon, as you prefer. For a change, try adding 300ml/½ pt dry cider to the cooking water. Any leftover bacon can, of course, be served cold.

Serves 6-8

1.35kg/3 lb bacon joint, such as gammon, collar or forehock
1 large onion, thickly sliced
1 large carrot, thickly sliced
2 celery sticks, roughly chopped
6 black peppercorns
4 whole cloves
2 bay leaves (optional)

Parsley Sauce:

15g/½ oz butter
15g/½ oz plain flour
300ml/½ pt milk
2-3 tbsp finely chopped fresh parsley
salt and freshly ground pepper

1. Put the bacon into a large saucepan and cover well with cold water. Heat slowly until the water comes to the boil. Drain off and discard the water.

2. To the pan, add the onion, carrot, celery, peppercorns, cloves and bay leaves (optional). Add sufficient water to cover the bacon.

3. Heat slowly until the water comes to the boil. Using a slotted spoon, skim the surface if necessary. Cover and cook very gently for about 1 hour 20 minutes (calculated on 20 minutes per 450g/1 lb plus an extra 20 minutes).

4. Towards the end of the cooking time, make the parsley sauce. Put the butter, flour, milk and parsley into a saucepan. Cook over medium heat, whisking continuously, until the sauce comes to the boil and thickens. Continue cooking very gently for 1-2 minutes. Season to taste with salt and pepper.

5. Lift the bacon on to a warm serving plate and cut off the rind. Serve it sliced with the parsley sauce.

To microwave the Parsley Sauce:

1. Put the flour, milk and parsley into a bowl or jug. Whisk well, then add the butter. Cook on HIGH for about 3 minutes, whisking frequently, or until the sauce comes to the boil and thickens. Continue cooking on MED-LOW for 1-2 minutes. Season to taste with salt and pepper.

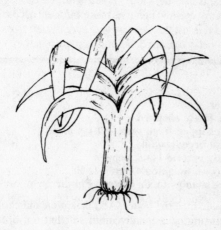

Roast Goose with Sage and Onion Stuffing and Apples

It is said that if you eat goose on Michaelmas Day (September 29th) you will have good luck and prosperity for the year ahead – "whoever eats goose on Michaelmas Day shall never lack money for his debts to pay". Goose is at its best in late September, which is also the time of apple harvesting, so it makes sense that the two are served together. The apples also help to offset the richness of the meat. Since the goose season lasts until December it has also become traditional Christmas fare. Geese were (and still are) farmed in the East of England and, in particular, East Anglia. Before the arrival of railways, large herds would be fattened up and their feet covered in tar before being driven, on foot, to fairs as far away as Nottingham and London.

When buying a goose, allow about 675g/1½ lb per person. Roast goose is also delicious served with red cabbage or apple sauce. Creamy mashed potatoes make the ideal accompaniment. (Incidentally, don't throw away the fat collected from the roasting goose – use it to roast deliciously crispy potatoes.)

Serves 8

25g/1 oz butter
1 large onion, finely chopped
1 tbsp finely chopped fresh sage or 1 tsp dried
175g/6 oz fresh breadcrumbs
salt and freshly ground black pepper
oven-ready goose, weighing 4-5kg/9-11 lb
5 crisp apples, such as Cox's Orange Pippin

1. In a saucepan, melt the butter. Add the onion and cook for about 5 minutes, stirring occasionally, until soft but not brown. Remove from the heat and stir in the sage and then the breadcrumbs. Season with salt and pepper.

2. Remove any fat from inside the goose. Using a fork, prick the skin all over then rub it with salt. Spoon the stuffing into the neck end of the bird and, with a small skewer, seal the skin over the opening. Weigh the goose, then place it on a rack in a roasting tin containing 150ml/¼ pt cold water. Cover the breast of the bird with foil.

3. Cook in a preheated oven at 200°C/400°F/Gas 6 for 15 minutes per 450g/1 lb plus an extra 15 minutes.

4. About 30 minutes before the end of cooking, lift out the goose and the rack and carefully drain the fat from the tin, leaving the sediment and juices behind. Halve the apples and remove their cores, then cut each half into four wedges. Put into the roasting tin, stirring to coat them lightly with the goose juices. Replace the rack with the goose on top. Remove the foil.

5. Continue cooking at 200°C/400°F/Gas 6 for the final 30 minutes, turning the apples over half way, until the goose is crisp and golden brown.

Roast Turkey with Stuffing and Sauce

Turkeys were first brought to Britain in the 16th century from North and Central America, via Mexico. As a 'speciality' they soon became the centrepiece of festive dinner tables and took over from boar's head, bustard and peacock at Christmas. Turkeys are now widely available in this country. For best flavour, look for the Cambridge, the Norfolk, the American Bronze, the Cambridge Bronze, the Kelly Bronze and the famous Norfolk Black.

Turkey consists of two types of meat – the delicate breast meat which can easily overcook and dry out and the darker leg meat which needs longer cooking to tenderise it. In the method below, the breast meat is kept moist by spreading butter under the skin which is then covered with bacon rashers during cooking. Fresh lemon and onion inserted in the main cavity of the turkey impart extra flavour to the bird and its juices. Put stuffing in to the neck end only.

Accompaniments for turkey include cranberry sauce (page 75), bread sauce (page 74), thin gravy (I like to use the juices from the roasting tin, bubbled up with some stock and port), small sausages and crispy bacon rolls.

An oven-ready turkey weighing 2.3-3.6kg/5-8 lb serves 6-10
one weighing 3.6-5kg/8-11 lb serves 10-15
one weighing 5-6.8kg/11-15 lb serves 15-20

1 lemon, cut into quarters
1 small onion, cut into quarters
oven-ready turkey (see above)
stuffing (see recipes on pages 72 and 73)
115g/4 oz soft butter
oil
streaky bacon rashers
freshly ground black pepper

1. Push the lemon and onion quarters into the main (not the neck) cavity of the turkey. Press the stuffing into the neck end and secure the flap of skin over the opening (use small skewers). Ease your fingers under the breast skin, lifting it gently and taking care not to break it, to make a large pocket. Insert the butter between the skin and breast meat and gently press the skin down on to it,

spreading it evenly over the breast (don't worry if it's not perfectly smooth).

2. Weigh the turkey and calculate the cooking time: 2-2½ hours for 2.3-3.6kg/5-8 lb, 3-4 hours for 3.6-5kg/8-11 lb, 3½-5 hours for 5-6.8kg/11-15 lb. Allow an extra 20-30 minutes for the turkey to stand and rest after cooking (carving will be much easier as a result).

3. Put the turkey in a roasting tin, brush it all over with oil and season it with pepper. Arrange bacon rashers over the breast area to completely cover it. Cover loosely with foil.

4. Cook in a preheated oven at 180°C/350°F/Gas 4 for the calculated time, basting occasionally and removing the foil ¾-1 hour before the end of cooking. To check that the bird is cooked thoroughly, insert a skewer into the thickest (inner) part of the thigh – the juices should run clear, not pink.

5. Discard the bacon rashers if they have become too tough to eat. Put the turkey on to a serving plate, cover with foil and leave to stand for 20-30 minutes before carving. This gives you time to make gravy and complete last-minute preparations (such as cooking small sausages and bacon rolls, crisping up roast potatoes, draining vegetables).

Stuffings for Turkey

> Quantities are for a 2.3-3.6kg/5-8 lb oven-ready turkey. Double the quantities for larger birds.

Parsley and Lemon

25g/1 oz butter
1 medium onion, finely chopped
115g/4 oz fresh breadcrumbs
3 tbsp finely chopped fresh parsley
finely grated rind of 1 lemon
salt and freshly ground black pepper
1 medium egg, lightly beaten

1. In a saucepan, melt the butter and add the onion. Cook over medium heat for about 8 minutes, stirring occasionally, or until very soft but not brown. (Alternatively, microwave the butter and onion on HIGH for about 5 minutes, stirring once, until very soft.)

2. Remove from the heat and stir in the breadcrumbs, parsley and lemon. Season with salt and pepper. Stir in the egg.

Sage and Onion

25g/1 oz butter
1 large onion, finely chopped
1 tbsp chopped fresh sage or 1 tsp dried
115g/4 oz fresh breadcrumbs
55g/2 oz medium oatmeal
salt and freshly ground pepper

1. In a saucepan, melt the butter and add the onion. Cook over medium heat for about 10 minutes, stirring occasionally, or until very soft but not brown. (Alternatively, microwave the butter and onion on HIGH for about 5 minutes, stirring once, until very soft.)

2. Remove from the heat and stir in the remaining ingredients.

Walnut, Orange and Thyme

25g/1 oz butter
1 medium onion, finely chopped
115g/4 oz fresh breadcrumbs
25g/1 oz finely chopped walnuts
finely grated rind and juice of 1 large orange
1 tbsp chopped fresh thyme leaves or 1 tsp dried
salt and freshly ground black pepper

1. In a saucepan, melt the butter and add the onion. Cook over medium heat for about 8 minutes, stirring occasionally, or until very soft but not brown. (Alternatively, microwave the butter and onion on HIGH for about 5 minutes, stirring once, until very soft.)

2. Remove from the heat and stir in the remaining ingredients.

Bread Sauce

Sauces made with breadcrumbs date back to medieval times. Bread Sauce can be made in advance and reheated gently before serving with turkey or other roast poultry.

Serves 6

1 small onion, thinly sliced
1 bay leaf
6 black peppercorns
2 cloves
good pinch of grated nutmeg
400ml/14 fl oz milk
55g/2 oz fresh white breadcrumbs
salt and freshly milled pepper
25g/1 oz butter

1. Put the onion into a saucepan with the bay leaf, peppercorns, cloves, nutmeg and milk. Heat slowly until the mixture comes to the boil.

2. Cover and leave to stand for 10-15 minutes, to allow the flavours to infuse into the milk.

3. Strain the milk and return it to the pan. Stir in the breadcrumbs and seasoning.

4. Cover and simmer gently for about 10 minutes, stirring occasionally until the sauce is thick and creamy. Stir in the butter.

To microwave:
1. Put the onion into a casserole with the bay leaf, peppercorns, cloves, nutmeg and milk. Cook uncovered on **HIGH** for about 3 minutes or until the mixture comes to the boil.

2. Cover and leave to stand for 10-15 minutes, to allow the flavours to infuse into the milk.

3. Strain the milk and return it to the casserole. Stir in the breadcrumbs.

4. Cover and cook on **MEDIUM** for about 5 minutes, stirring occasionally, or until the sauce is thick and creamy. Stir in the butter.

Cranberry Sauce

Make this in advance and serve warm or cold with roast turkey. For a more interesting flavour, use orange juice to cook the cranberries. Alternatively, stir a tablespoon or two of port into the cooked cranberry sauce.

Serves 6

225g/8 oz cranberries
300ml/½ pt water or orange juice
175-225g/6-8 oz sugar

1. Put the cranberries into a saucepan with the water or juice. Cook over medium heat until the mixture comes to the boil, then simmer gently for about 10 minutes or until the cranberries have burst open.
2. Add the sugar and simmer gently, stirring occasionally, until it has dissolved.

To microwave:
1. Put the cranberries into a large casserole with the water or juice. Cook on HIGH for about 3 minutes or until the mixture comes to the boil. Cook on MEDIUM for about 5 minutes or until the cranberries have burst open.
2. Stir in the sugar and cook on MEDIUM for about 5 minutes, stirring occasionally, or until the sugar has dissolved.

Fidget Pie

Ham, potato, apple and onion are the ingredients which make up this speciality from the Midlands. Fidget Pie is strongly linked to harvest time – in Shropshire particularly – when the workers would look forward to eating it after a long day in the fields. It is similar to the Devonshire Squab Pie, which also combines savoury and sweet flavours but usually contains beef, mutton or pork. For the recipe below, choose lean gammon; the stock can be replaced with wine or dry cider.

Serves 4

225g/8 oz potatoes, peeled and thinly sliced
350g/12 oz gammon, rind and fat removed, cut into small cubes
1 large onion, thinly sliced
2 medium cooking apples, total weight about 350g/12 oz
150ml/¼ pt ham, chicken or vegetable stock
1 tsp sugar
½ tsp dried thyme
freshly ground black pepper
175g/6 oz shortcrust pastry
beaten egg, to glaze

1. Arrange half the potatoes in the base of a 850ml/1½ pt pie dish. Add half the gammon, onion and apples. Repeat the layers, using the remaining potatoes, gammon, onion and apples.

2. Into the stock, stir the sugar and thyme. Season with black pepper. Pour the mixture over the filling in the pie dish.

3. On a lightly floured surface, roll out the pastry until it is large enough to cover the dish. Lay the pastry on top of the filling and trim the edges. Brush with beaten egg and make a small slit in the centre.

4. Cook in a preheated oven at 180°C/350°F/Gas 4 for about 50 minutes or until the pastry is golden brown and the filling is cooked.

Duck with Cumberland Sauce

Mrs Beeton considered the Aylesbury duck to have the best eating qualities. In those days, they were reared intensively in people's homes and transported to London for sale. Other British-produced ducks to look out for include Gressingham and Lunesdale. When buying, you need to allow at least 450g/1 lb per person. Ducks tend to have a thick layer of fat, most of which needs to drain off the bird during cooking. The recipe below works well with all types of duck and the sweet-and-sour flavour of the sauce goes well with the richness of the meat.

Serves 4

oven-ready duckling, weighing about 2.25kg/5 lb
salt and freshly milled pepper
1 orange, quartered
finely grated rind and juice of 1 orange and 1 lemon
2 tsp cornflour
5 tbsp port
2 tbsp brandy
4 tbsp redcurrant jelly

1. Wash and dry the duckling thoroughly. With a fork, prick the skin all over, then season with salt and pepper. Push the orange quarters into the cavity (you may need to cut them smaller). Put the duck, breast side up, on a rack standing in a roasting tin.

2. Cook in a preheated oven at 180°C/350°F/Gas 4 for about 2½ hours until crisp and cooked through (the juices should run clear when the thickest part of the leg is pierced with a skewer). Do not cover or baste during cooking, but occasionally you may need to spoon or pour off the fat which collects in the roasting tin.

3. Transfer the duck to a serving plate, carve into quarters and keep warm.

4. Pour off the fat from the roasting tin, leaving the sediment and just 1 tbsp fat behind. Add the rind and juice of the orange and lemon, then whisk in the cornflour. Add the port, brandy and redcurrant jelly.

5. Cook over medium-low heat, stirring, until the sauce comes to the boil and thickens slightly, and the jelly has melted. Adjust the seasoning if necessary.

6. Serve the sauce with the duck.

Venison Casserole

The rich, gamy flavour of venison is probably best appreciated in the Scottish Highlands where wild deer have been hunted for hundreds of years. Wild venison comes from red, fallow or roe deer. In the past, it has been an expensive 'luxury' meat, often served to the 'privileged' classes. These days, venison farms have become very popular and it is now widely available across the country.

All venison is very lean and needs careful cooking if it is not to dry out.

Serves 4

150ml/¼ pt red wine
3 tbsp olive oil
1 garlic clove, crushed
8 juniper berries
8 black peppercorns
4 cloves
1 cinnamon stick
3 fresh thyme sprigs
3 fresh parsley sprigs
900g/2 lb stewing venison, cut into cubes
2 medium onions, sliced
4 lean streaky bacon rashers, chopped
1 medium carrot, sliced
2 tbsp plain flour
150ml/¼ pt game or chicken stock
3 tbsp redcurrant jelly
salt and freshly ground black pepper
3 tbsp chopped fresh parsley

1. Put the wine into a bowl with 1 tbsp oil. Add the garlic, juniper, peppercorns, cloves, cinnamon and herbs. Stir in the venison, pushing it into the marinade. Cover and leave to stand overnight in a cool place, stirring occasionally if possible.

2. Using a slotted spoon, lift the venison from the marinade. Strain and reserve the marinade.

3. Heat the remaining oil in a flameproof casserole and quickly brown the venison in small batches, lifting it out on to a plate.

4. Add the onions, bacon and carrot to the pan and cook for 5-10 minutes, stirring occasionally, until the vegetables are soft and the bacon begins to brown. Add the flour and cook, stirring, for 1-2 minutes. Remove from the heat and gradually stir in the reserved marinade and the stock. Add the redcurrant jelly and seasoning. Stir in the venison and its juices.

5. Cook over medium heat, stirring occasionally, until the mixture comes to the boil and thickens slightly.

6. Cover and cook in a preheated oven at 170°C/325°F/Gas 3 for 2 hours or more until the venison is tender.

7. Stir in the chopped parsley just before serving.

Stew and Dumplings

There are many variations of this comforting dish. I have given a classic version for beef below, but do try other variations. Try using brown ale in place of stock, or replace half the stock with cider or wine. A tablespoon of Worcestershire sauce will really pep it up, as will one or two spoonfuls of horseradish sauce or your favourite mustard. Of course, you don't have to use beef – why not use lamb, pork or chicken with the appropriate stock and adjusting the cooking time accordingly? As for the dumplings, instead of herbs, these could be flavoured with grated mature cheese, seeds (such as caraway) or paprika. Make the dumplings just before you add them to the stew. Serve the stew in shallow bowls with chunks of fresh crusty bread to mop up the delicious juices.

Serves 4-6

3 tbsp oil
900g/2 lb lean stewing steak, cut into cubes
2 large onions, each one cut lengthways into about 8 wedges
2 celery sticks, thickly sliced
2 large carrots, thickly sliced
2 medium turnips, cut into cubes
2 tbsp flour
850ml/1½ pt beef stock
2 tbsp tomato purée
salt and freshly ground black pepper

Dumplings:
175g/6 oz self-raising flour
85g/3 oz shredded suet
2 tbsp finely chopped fresh herbs, such as parsley or thyme or a mixture
salt and freshly ground black pepper

1. Heat the oil in a large heavy-base saucepan. When hot, add about one quarter of the beef and cook over high heat, stirring occasionally, until browned on all sides. Using a slotted spoon, lift out on to a plate. Repeat the process with the remaining meat.

2. Lower the heat and add the onions, celery, carrots and turnips. Cook over medium heat, stirring occasionally, for about 10 minutes or until they begin to soften and turn light golden brown. With the slotted spoon, lift these out too.

3. Add the flour to the remaining oil in the pan and cook, stirring (and scraping up the sediment which will have stuck to the bottom of the pan) until light golden brown. Gradually stir in the stock, then add the tomato purée and a little seasoning. Heat, stirring, until the mixture comes to the boil and thickens slightly.

4. Return the meat (with its juices) and the vegetables to the pan. Cover and simmer very gently for 2-2½ hours, stirring occasionally, until the beef is tender.

5. To make the dumplings, sift the flour into a bowl and stir in the suet, herb(s) and seasoning. With a flat-blade knife, stir in sufficient water to make a soft dough. Divide the mixture into 18 balls.

6. Arrange the dumplings on top of the stew, cover and simmer gently for 15-20 minutes until they are well risen and cooked.

Pheasant Casserole with Port and Orange

Pheasants can be seen in many parts of the country, the males drawing our attention with their colourful plumage. Hen birds have brown and cream feathers, are generally more tender, and normally provide two portions. Male birds usually feed three. This recipe is an ideal way of cooking pheasant which, at the end of the season especially, can be a little tough and the meat dry (though the flavour is always good).

Serves 4-6

25g/1 oz butter
225g/8 oz lean streaky bacon, cut into 1cm/½ in pieces
2 oven-ready pheasants
2 celery sticks, thinly sliced
150ml/¼ pt chicken stock
150ml/¼ pt port
finely grated rind and juice of 1 orange
bouquet garni
salt and freshly ground black pepper
1 tbsp cornflour
1 tbsp orange marmalade (optional)

1. Heat the butter in a flameproof casserole, large enough to hold the pheasants side by side, and add the bacon. Cook over medium heat for about 5 minutes, or until the fat runs out of the bacon and it is crisp. Using a slotted spoon, transfer the bacon to a plate.
2. Add the pheasants to the fat in the casserole and cook quickly until brown on all sides. Add the celery, stock, port, orange rind and juice, and bouquet garni. Season with salt and pepper. Heat until the liquid just comes to the boil.
3. Cover and cook in a preheated oven at 170°C/325°F/Gas 3 for 1-1½ hours or until the pheasants are tender.
4. Lift the pheasants on to a serving plate, carve into halves or quarters and keep warm.
5. Remove and discard the bouquet garni. Mix the cornflour with a little cold water to make a smooth paste. Whisk in a couple of spoonfuls of the hot stock, then stir the mixture into the casserole. Cook over medium-low heat, stirring until the sauce comes to the boil. Add the marmalade (optional) and adjust the seasoning if necessary.
6. Serve the sauce with the pheasant.

Lancashire Hotpot

This northern recipe was created to 'make a little go a long way'. It's a simple, layered dish that makes a delicious and warming winter meal out of three basic ingredients – lamb chops, potatoes and onion. Years ago, it would probably have contained oysters, which were cheap fare. Housewives would take their hotpots to the cooling bread ovens at the end of the day and leave them to cook for several hours. To the basic recipe below, I sometimes add a carrot or two, or some sliced leeks or mushrooms. If time allows, browning the lamb in hot fat, before layering up the ingredients, produces even more flavour.

Serves 4

900g/2 lb potatoes, thinly sliced
salt and freshly ground black pepper
8 lean best end of neck lamb chops, trimmed of excess fat
2 lamb's kidneys, skinned, cores removed and sliced
2 medium onions, thinly sliced into rings
425ml/¾ pt lamb stock or vegetable stock
25g/1 oz butter
2 fresh rosemary sprigs (optional)

1. Arrange one third of the potatoes in an ovenproof casserole dish and season with salt and pepper. Lay four chops on top with half of the kidney pieces and half of the onion slices. Repeat with a second layer of potatoes, seasoning, chops, kidney and onion. Arrange the remaining potatoes in overlapping circles on top. Pour the stock over and dot with the butter. Top with the rosemary sprigs (optional).

2. Cover and cook at 180°C/350°F/Gas 4 for 1½ hours.

3. Remove cover, discard the rosemary if used and continue cooking at 220°/425°F/Gas 7 for 20-30 minutes or until the potatoes are well browned.

Kedgeree

Kitcheree or Kedgeree is actually a spicy Indian dish containing rice, onions and lentils. The version below was supposedly developed as a breakfast dish by the British army. The spices were left out and pieces of smoked haddock were added. These days, we are more likely to serve Kedgeree as a lunch or supper dish.

Serves 4

175g/6 oz basmati rice, washed
salt and freshly ground black pepper
450g/1 lb smoked haddock fillet
2 eggs, hard-boiled and shelled
50g/1¾ g butter
2 tbsp chopped fresh parsley

1. Cook the rice in plenty of salted boiling water, following packet instructions, for about 12 minutes or until tender. Drain and rinse under cold water.

2. Meanwhile, put the haddock into a frying pan and add enough water to just cover it. Heat until the water just starts to simmer, cover and cook gently for 5 minutes. Remove from the heat and leave to stand for about 5 minutes, by which time the fish should be cooked through. Drain the haddock and flake the fish, discarding skin and bones.

3. Chop one egg and thinly slice the other.

4. Melt the butter in the cleaned frying pan. Add the cooked rice and fish and the chopped egg. Season to taste. Cook gently, stirring occasionally, for about 5 minutes or until everything is hot.

5. Scatter the parsley over the top and serve, topped with the egg slices.

To microwave:

1. Put the rice into a large casserole and pour over 300ml/½ pt *boiling* water. Stir well. Cook, uncovered, on HIGH for 8-10 minutes or until just tender. Drain and rinse under cold water.

2. Put the haddock in a shallow dish, cover and cook on MEDIUM for about 12 minutes or until just cooked. Leave to stand for 5 minutes then flake the fish, discarding skin and bones.

3. Chop one egg and thinly slice the other.

4. Put the butter into the cleaned casserole and heat on HIGH until melted. Gently stir in the cooked rice and haddock and the chopped egg. Season to taste. Cook on MEDIUM for about 5 minutes, stirring occasionally, or until hot.

5. Scatter the parsley over and serve, topped with the egg slices.

Fish Pie

Though we may think of it as an 'old fashioned' dish, fish pie with its topping of mashed potatoes is in fact a relatively new recipe. Serve it with a green vegetable.

Serves 4

**675g/1½ lb British floury potatoes, such as King Edward or
  Desirée, peeled and cut into cubes**
85g/3 oz butter
425ml/¾ pt milk, plus 4 tbsp
225g/8 oz skinless white fish, such as haddock or cod
225g/8 oz smoked haddock or cod
25g/1 oz flour
pinch of cayenne pepper
salt and freshly ground pepper
1 bunch of spring onions, sliced
225g/8 oz peeled, cooked prawns
2 tbsp finely chopped fresh parsley
2 eggs, hard-boiled, shells removed and thinly sliced

1. Cook the potatoes in a saucepan of salted water for about 20 minutes or until tender. Drain and mash with 25g/1oz butter and the 4 tbsp milk.

2. Put the white and smoked fish in a frying pan and pour the remaining 425ml/¾ pt milk over. Cook over medium heat until the milk just comes to the boil. Cover and cook gently for about 8 minutes or until the fish is just cooked. Carefully lift the fish out of the pan and break it into large flakes, discarding any bones.

3. In a saucepan, heat 25g/1 oz butter until melted. Stir in the flour and cook gently, stirring for 1-2 minutes. Remove the pan from the heat and gradually stir in the cooking liquid from the fish. Cook over medium heat, stirring, until the sauce comes to the boil and thickens. Add the cayenne and season to taste with salt and pepper.

4. Into the sauce, stir the fish flakes and their juices, onions, prawns and parsley. Spoon the mixture into a 1.2 litre/2 pt ovenproof dish.

5. Arrange the egg slices over the fish mixture. Spoon the potato in

an even layer on top and rough the surface with a fork. Melt the remaining 25g/1 oz butter and drizzle it over the potato topping.

6. Cook in a preheated oven at 200°C/400°F/Gas 6 for about 30 minutes or until golden brown.

To microwave:

1. Put the potatoes into a large casserole with 4 tbsp water. Cover and cook on HIGH for about 10 minutes, stirring occasionally, until tender. Drain and mash with 25g/1 oz butter and the 4 tbsp milk.

2. Put the white and smoked fish in a casserole and pour over half the milk. Cover and cook for about 4 minutes or until the fish is just cooked. Carefully lift the fish out of the dish and break it into large flakes, discarding any bones.

3. Put the flour into a bowl or jug and whisk in the cooking liquid from the fish and the remaining milk. Add 25g/1 oz butter. Cook on HIGH for about 3 minutes, whisking frequently, until the sauce comes to the boil and thickens. Add the cayenne and season to taste with salt and pepper.

4. Into the sauce, stir the fish flakes and their juices, onions, prawns and parsley. Spoon the mixture into a 1.2 litre/2 pt flameproof dish.

5. Arrange the egg slices over the fish mixture. Spoon the potato in an even layer on top and rough the surface with a fork. Melt the remaining 25g/1 oz butter and drizzle it over the potato topping.

6. Cook on MEDIUM for about 10 minutes or until bubbling hot, then brown the top under a hot grill.

Skate with Black Butter

The 'black' butter that accompanies the fish should be a deep golden colour, speckled with dark green capers. Skate, though it may not look it, is a meaty fish. The bones are long, but gelatinous rather than sharp, and the cooked fish slides off them with ease. Buy skate which has had its dark skin removed. Capers are available preserved in vinegar (drain and rinse before using) or in salt. I prefer the salted version – soak them in plenty of cold water for ½-1 hour and drain before using.

Serves 4

4 pieces of skate wings, total weight 675-900g/1½-2 lb
1 small onion, thinly sliced
salt and freshly ground pepper
55g/2 oz butter
1 tbsp capers
2 tbsp wine vinegar
1 tbsp chopped fresh parsley (optional)

1. Put the skate in a frying pan with the onion and a little salt. Cover with water and heat slowly until it comes just to the boil. Cook very gently for 10-15 minutes until the fish is just cooked.

2. Meanwhile, melt the butter in a small saucepan and cook gently until it is golden brown. Stir in the capers, vinegar and parsley (optional). Heat until the mixture just bubbles.

3. Using a slotted spoon, transfer the fish to warm serving plates, discarding the liquid and onion.

4. Pour the caper sauce over and serve immediately.

Mackerel with Gooseberry Sauce

Gooseberries have been used in cooking since the 1800s and maybe even earlier. Both gooseberries and mackerel come into season in early summer so it seems natural that they should have been paired together. The tartness of the gooseberries is ideal alongside the oily richness of mackerel. Herrings suit this treatment too.

Serves 4

15g/½ oz butter
225g/8 oz gooseberries, thawed if frozen, topped and tailed
about 1 tbsp sugar (optional)
¼ tsp grated nutmeg
1 medium egg, beaten
salt and pepper
4 mackerel, each weighing 225-350g/8-12 oz, cleaned and heads
removed

1. Melt the butter in a saucepan and add the gooseberries. Cover and cook gently for about 10 minutes, stirring occasionally, or until the gooseberries are soft. Tip the mixture into a food processor and purée until smooth. Pass the purée through a nylon sieve and discard the tiny pips. Return the purée to the pan and stir in the sugar (add only enough to just offset any harshness – it depends on the gooseberries – they may not need sweetening at all). Stir in the nutmeg, egg and seasoning.

2. Season the mackerel with salt and pepper, inside and out. With a sharp knife, make two or three slashes on each side of the fish. Put under a hot grill for 5-10 minutes each side until the skin is crisp and the fish is cooked through.

3. Heat the gooseberry sauce gently, stirring continuously, without allowing it to boil.

4. Serve the mackerel with the sauce.

To microwave the gooseberries:
1. Put the butter and gooseberries into a casserole, cover and cook on HIGH for about 6 minutes, stirring once or twice, until soft. Continue as above.

Trout with Bacon

Here is a typical Celtic combination of ingredients. The Welsh name for this recipe is *Brithyll A Cig Moch*. Usually, the bacon is simply laid in the bottom of an ovenproof dish, with the trout on top. I like to wrap the bacon around the fish – use thin rashers of home-cured bacon if you can get it. In place of parsley, I often use sage leaves, placing a couple between the bacon and the fish on each trout. This recipe is great for the barbecue too.

Serves 4

4 trout, each weighing about 225g/8 oz, cleaned
salt and freshly ground pepper
2 tbsp finely chopped fresh parsley
4 lemon slices
8 lean streaky bacon rashers, rinds removed

1. Season the trout inside and out. Divide half the parsley between the fish cavities and insert a lemon slice into each. Wrap two bacon rashers, spiral fashion, around each trout. Arrange them in a shallow ovenproof dish (try and make sure that the ends of the bacon lie underneath the trout – to prevent them unwinding).

2. Cook in a preheated oven at 180°/350°F/Gas 4 for about 20 minutes until the fish is tender.

3. Sprinkle with the remaining parsley and serve.

Fish and Chips

Both the North and South claim to have first served deep-fried fish with chips. I shall leave the debate to you but one thing is certain – the meal known as 'fish and chips' has become a national institution. Northerners seem to prefer haddock, while Southerners (and Londoners in particular) like cod and huss. Everyone agrees that salt and vinegar are the best accompaniments.

Serves 2

Batter:
100g/3¾ oz self-raising flour
¼ tsp baking powder
¼ tsp salt

oil for deep frying
550g/1¼ lb potatoes, peeled and cut into chips
. 2 white fish fillets, each weighing 175-225g/6-8 oz

1. To make the batter, sift the flour, baking powder and salt into a bowl. Beat in sufficient cold water, a little at a time, until the batter is smooth and of a thick pouring consistency. Leave to stand. `

2. Meanwhile, heat the oil in a deep-fat fryer to 190°C/375°F (a chip dropped into the oil should rise immediately, bubbling to the surface). Using kitchen paper or a clean teatowel, pat the potato chips dry. Carefully lower the chips into the hot oil and cook for 5-8 minutes or until they just begin to brown. With a slotted spoon or wire basket, lift the chips out. Wait for the oil to return to temperature, then lower them back into the oil and cook for about 3 minutes or until crisp and golden. Lift out and put into a warm dish lined with kitchen paper. Keep warm.

3. Heat the oil until it again reaches190°C/375°F. Dip the fish in the batter, coating it well. Immediately lower the fish (skin side down to prevent it curling) into the hot oil. Cook for 3-4 minutes or until the batter begins to brown. Turn the fish over and continue cooking for about 2 minutes or until crisp and golden brown all over. Lift out and drain on kitchen paper.

4. Serve the fish immediately with the chips.

Rabbit Casserole

Rabbit was probably at its most popular in the Middle Ages. Later, in the 1800s, when rabbit skin was sought after for hats and gloves, it became a profitable trade. Since then, its popularity has fluctuated. Wild rabbit has a stronger flavour than commercially bred and the latter has a paler flesh which looks similar to chicken. In fact, this recipe also works well using chicken thighs. It has always been traditional to cook rabbit with plenty of herbs; the idea of adding Dijon mustard is more recent. I like to serve this accompanied with hunks of fresh crusty bread.

Serves 4

1 large rabbit, jointed, or 8 small rabbit joint
2 tbsp flour, well seasoned with salt and freshly ground black pepper
2 tbsp oil
15g/½ oz butter
1 large onion, thinly sliced
1 plump garlic clove, crushed
225g/8 oz carrots, thinly sliced
225g/8 oz waxy potatoes, such as British-grown Cara, Estima or Wilja, cut into small dice
600ml/1 pt chicken stock
300ml/½ pt dry white wine
2 tbsp Dijon mustard
1 tbsp mixed dried herbs

1. Coat the rabbit pieces in the seasoned flour.

2. Heat the oil and butter in a large frying pan. Add the rabbit and cook quickly until golden brown on all sides. Transfer to a large casserole.

3. Add the onion, garlic and carrots to the frying pan and cook over medium heat for about 10 minutes, stirring frequently, until they begin to soften and turn golden brown. Add to the casserole with the potatoes.

4. Mix together the remaining ingredients and add to the casserole. Cover.

5. Cook in a preheated oven at 150°C/300°F/Gas 2 for 1½-2 hours or until the rabbit is tender.

Beef in Stout

It is the roasted malt or barley in stout that gives this dish (Irish in origin) its rich colour and almost-bitter flavour. I usually use Guinness – it gives the sauce a really smooth, rich texture. The ingredients are cooked gently and slowly until the beef nearly falls apart. Don't be tempted to leave out the sugar – if you do, the flavour will not be nearly so good. Sometimes, in place of the sugar, I add about 175g/6 oz chopped ready-to-eat prunes – they melt into the sauce during cooking. Wonderful!

Serves 4-6

900g/2 lb lean stewing steak, cut into 5cm/2 in cubes
3 tbsp flour, seasoned with salt and freshly ground black pepper
3 tbsp oil
2 large onions, thinly sliced
2 celery sticks, thinly sliced
300ml/½ pt stout
2 tbsp tomato purée
1 tsp dried mixed herbs
1 tbsp dark muscovado sugar
225g/8 oz button mushrooms, halved

1. Coat the beef cubes in the seasoned flour.

2. Heat the oil in a large, flameproof casserole. Add the meat, about one third at a time, and cook quickly until browned on all sides. With a slotted spoon, lift out on to a plate. Repeat with the remaining beef.

3. To the pan, add the onions and celery. Cook over medium heat for about 10 minutes, stirring frequently, until they begin to soften.

4. Return the meat to the pan and add the stout, scraping up any sediment which is stuck to the bottom of the dish. Stir in the remaining ingredients and cover.

5. Cook in a preheated oven at 170°C/325°F/Gas 3 for about 2-2½ hours or until the beef is meltingly tender.

4

PUDDINGS & DESSERTS

Here you will find some of your favourite 'old-fashioned' puddings – the ones which always make your family and friends heave nostalgic sighs and ask for second helpings.

Apple and Blackberry Crumble

Fruit crumbles are not only delicious, they are one of the easiest desserts to make. Preparing the crumble mixture is similar to making pastry, but without the mixing and rolling. Vary the fruits according to what is available – plums, rhubarb, gooseberries, peaches, raspberries. The crumble mixture can be made with wholemeal flour and brown or demerara sugar. Try adding a little spice to the flour before rubbing in the butter (ground cinnamon, ginger, nutmeg, coriander or mixed spice), or add a spoonful or two of desiccated coconut (a favourite in my family) to crumble mix with the sugar in step 1. Serve it warm with thick yogurt, cream or custard.

Serves 4

115g/4 oz plain flour
55g/2 oz butter
115g/4 oz caster sugar
450g/1 lb Bramley apples, peeled, cored and thinly sliced
115g/4 oz blackberries, thawed if frozen

1. Sift the flour into a bowl and rub in the butter until the mixture resembles fine crumbs (alternatively, this can be done in a food processor). Stir in 55g/2 oz sugar.

2. Arrange the apples and blackberries in a 1.2 litre/2 pt ovenproof dish, sprinkling the layers with the remaining 55g/2 oz sugar.

3. Spoon the crumble mixture evenly over the fruit.

4. Cook in a preheated oven at 180°C/350°F/Gas 4 for about 40 minutes or until the top is golden (not dark) brown and the fruit is bubbling and soft.

To microwave:

1. Follow step 1 above.

2. Put the apples and sugar into a casserole, cover and cook on HIGH for about 4 minutes, stirring once, until the apples are soft. Stir in the blackberries. Tip the fruit mixture into a 20cm/8 in soufflé dish.

3. Spoon the crumble mixture evenly over the hot fruit.

4. Cook, uncovered, on MED-HIGH for about 8 minutes or until the topping is cooked at the centre. Leave to stand for 5 minutes before serving.

Apple Pie

'Of all the delicates that Britons try
To please the palate and delight the eye,
Of all the sev'ral kinds of sumptuous fare,
There is none that can with apple pie compare'

William King (1663-1712)

Since Elizabethan times, apple pie has been a traditional way to end a meal and it must now be an all-time favourite. My father, I know, would never forgive me if I were to omit his preferred choice of dessert. Try replacing a proportion of the apples with another fruit, such as fresh blackberries or blackcurrants, or dried fruit such as sultanas or chopped ready-to-eat apricots. Instead of ginger, add a pinch of ground cinnamon, cloves or mixed spice to the apples. I like to use a sweet pastry topping though you can, of course, use plain shortcrust pastry. Serve it warm with cream or custard.

Serves 6

Pastry:
200g/7 oz plain flour
25g/1 oz caster sugar
115g/4 oz chilled butter
1 medium egg, lightly beaten

Filling:
55g/2 oz sugar
¼ tsp ground ginger
900g/2 lb Bramley apples, peeled, cored and thinly sliced
caster sugar, for sprinkling

1. Sift the flour into a bowl and stir in the sugar (or mix them for 2-3 seconds in a food processor). Using your fingers, rub the butter into the flour mixture (or do this in the food processor) until the mixture resembles fine crumbs. Stir in the egg until the mixture clumps, then gather it together to make a smooth dough (or, in the processor, insert a plastic blade and mix until the dough gathers together in a ball). Wrap the pastry and allow it to 'relax' in the refrigerator for 30minutes.

2. Mix together the sugar and ginger. Arrange the apples in a 1.2 litre/2 pt pie dish, layering them with the sugar mixture. Add 1 tbsp water.

3. On a lightly floured surface, roll out the pastry to make a shape which is slightly larger than the dish. Brush the edges of the dish with water, cover with the pastry and, with a sharp knife, trim off the excess. Pinch a pattern around the edges of the pastry and make a small slit in the centre. Lightly brush the top with water and sprinkle with a little caster sugar.

4. Cook in a preheated oven at 190°C/375°F/Gas 5 for about 40 minutes or until the pastry is golden brown.

5. While the pie is still hot, sprinkle with more caster sugar.

Rice Pudding

This creamy dessert was always popular in farming areas where an abundance of milk was produced. In North Wales, rice pudding was traditionally served on a Sunday, after the family had been to chapel. I like it best made with full cream milk and the nutmeg freshly grated over the top. For best results, long slow cooking is the order of the day. If you want a really creamy pudding, stir in a couple of tablespoons of cream after the first 45 minutes cooking.

Serves 4

50g/1¾ oz pudding rice
25g/1 oz caster sugar
600ml/1 pt milk
few drops of vanilla essence
15g/½ oz butter
freshly grated nutmeg

1. Butter an 850ml/1½ pt ovenproof dish and add the rice and sugar. Stir in the milk and vanilla essence. Cut the butter into small pieces and dot over the top. Grate some nutmeg over the surface.

2. Cook in a preheated oven at 150°C/300°F/Gas 2 for about 2 hours (stir the pudding two or three times in the first 45 minutes) until the rice is tender and the top is brown.

To microwave:
1. Put the rice, sugar, milk, vanilla essence and butter into a large casserole. Grate in some nutmeg.

2. Cook on HIGH for about 6 minutes, stirring twice, or until the mixture comes to the boil. Cover and cook on MED-LOW for about 30 minutes, stirring occasionally, until the rice is tender and the pudding is creamy. If wished, spoon the pudding into a flameproof dish and lightly brown the top under a hot grill.

Jam Roly Poly

Jam Roly Poly brings fond memories of childhood to many a grandparent. When they were young, this pudding would have been steamed for hours in a pan on the hob. In this recipe, it is baked in the oven – much more convenient for most of us. This is another recipe which has reappeared on pub and restaurant menus. Make the suet crust pastry with beef or vegetarian suet. If you like, replace the jam with thick-cut marmalade. Serve the pudding hot – do not allow it to cool down. Thick custard is the ideal accompaniment.

Serves 4-6

175g/6 oz self-raising flour
¼ tsp salt
85g/3 oz shredded suet
6 tbsp jam
1 tsp finely grated lemon rind

1. Sift the flour and salt into a bowl and stir in the suet. Using a flat round-blade knife, stir in sufficient cold water to make a light, elastic dough. Use your hands to finish mixing it to a smooth ball which is suitable for rolling out.

2. On a lightly floured surface, roll out the pastry to make a rectangle measuring about 20cm x 30cm/8 in x12 in.

3. Spread the jam thickly on the pastry, leaving the edges free. Sprinkle the lemon rind over the jam. Lightly brush the edges with water and roll up from a short side. Seal the ends by pinching them together.

4. Wrap the roll loosely with baking paper, then with foil, twisting the ends to close them. Place the roll on a baking sheet.

5. Cook in a preheated oven at 180°C/350°F/Gas 4 for 30-40 minutes.

6. Unwrap carefully (take care not to burn yourself) and serve.

Jelly

Sweet jellies were originally set with melted shavings of antler (hartshorn) or isinglass (made from fish), with rosewater being the common flavouring. Today, we can buy sweet jelly tablets in almost any flavour imaginable, ready for melting in hot water before leaving to set. A jelly made with fresh fruit juice tastes so much better. If you prefer a vegetarian alternative to gelatine, use agar-agar, following the instructions on the packet. Try setting small pieces of fresh fruit in the jelly, but do not use pineapple, papaya or kiwi fruit – they contain an enzyme (papain) which breaks down the gelatine and prevents it setting. Serve jelly with cream or ice cream and some cooked and chilled fresh summer fruits.

Serves 4

11g packet powdered gelatine or 4 sheets of leaf gelatine
600ml/1 pt fresh fruit juice, such as orange, apple or mango

1. If using powdered gelatine, sprinkle it over 3 tbsp cold water and leave to soak for 5 minutes until 'spongy'. If using leaf gelatine, soak it in about 3 tbsp cold water for 10 minutes before using.

2. Heat half the fruit juice until hot but not boiling (do this on the hob or in the microwave). Quickly whisk the gelatine into the hot juice. Once it has dissolved, stir in the remaining cold juice.

3. Pour into a dish and chill for at least 4 hours until set.

4. About 45 minutes before serving, remove the jelly from the fridge (it will taste much better at room temperature).

Blancmange

Blancmange, or white pudding as it was called, is a concoction which dates back to the Middle Ages. It was the Victorians who made it into a hugely popular dessert. It could be made with gelatine, arrowroot or cornflour. Today, we can buy sachets of powder for making blancmange made up of cornflour with added flavours and colouring. The home-made version is still the best. Use this recipe to make vanilla, chocolate or coffee blancmange too – simply leave out the lemon rind and add 1 tsp vanilla essence, 55g/2 oz melted chocolate or 2 tbsp coffee essence at the end of step 2. Honey (about 2 tbsp) instead of sugar, imparts a lovely delicate flavour too. Blancmange is good served with a fruit purée and some crisp sweet biscuits.

Serves 4

3 tbsp cornflour
600ml/1 pt milk
a strip of lemon rind
40g/1½ oz caster sugar, or to taste

1. Blend the cornflour to a smooth paste with a little of the milk. On the hob or in the microwave, gently heat the remaining milk with the lemon rind until it just comes to the boil. Strain it on to the cornflour mixture, stirring well.

2. Heat the mixture (stirring continuously on the hob or frequently in the microwave) until it comes to the boil and thickens. Continue cooking gently for a further 1-2 minutes.

3. Stir in sugar to taste. Pour into a mould and chill until set.

4. Turn out onto a plate to serve.

Gooseberry Fool

The dessert banquets of the 16th century would be likely to contain at least one fruit fool. It seems to have slipped out of fashion recently, though it often appears under new (trendy) guises. It is one of the simplest desserts to make. If you like, use other fruits in place of the gooseberries, such as apples, blackberries, raspberries, rhubarb, redcurrants or blackcurrants. Sometimes, I replace half or all the cream with 150ml/¼ pt or 300ml/½ pt thick custard or thick yogurt. Serve this with crisp sweet biscuits.

Serves 4

450g/1 lb gooseberries, topped and tailed
115g/4 oz caster sugar, or to taste
350ml/12 fl oz double cream
mint leaves, to decorate (optional)

1. Put the gooseberries into a saucepan with 3 tbsp water. Cover and cook gently for about 10 minutes, stirring occasionally, until the fruit is soft. Stir in sugar to taste.

2. Tip the fruit into a processor and purée until smooth. If wished, push through a nylon sieve to remove the pips. Leave to cool completely.

3. Whip the cream to make soft peaks. Gradually fold in the fruit purée.

4. Spoon into serving glasses and chill.

5. Decorate with mint leaves (optional) to serve.

Eton Mess

The famous public school, Eton College, gave this simple but delicious dessert its name. It was, and maybe still is, served to parents and pupils at the College's annual picnic on prize-giving day. Eat this soon after making it, otherwise the meringue will melt into the cream (though it will still taste delicious).

Serves 4

450g/1 lb ripe strawberries
3-4 tbsp liqueur, such as kirsch or Grand Marnier
300ml/½ pt double or whipping cream
4 meringues or meringue baskets, crushed into small pieces

1. Reserve some strawberries for decoration. Slice the remainder into a bowl and sprinkle with the liqueur. Cover and refrigerate for about 2 hours.

2. Whip the cream to soft peaks. Fold in the sliced strawberries with their juices, together with the meringues.

3. Spoon into one large serving dish or four small ones. Decorate with the reserved strawberries and serve.

Whim Wham

In the 18th century, ''whim wham'' was said to be a Scottish term for light and fanciful. To see whether this boozy dish lives up to the description, try it for yourself.

Serves 4

25g/1 oz butter
40g/1½ oz blanched almonds
15g/½ oz caster sugar
20 sponge fingers
100ml/3½ fl oz Madeira or sweet sherry
2 tbsp brandy
finely grated rind and juice of 1 medium orange
150ml/¼ pt double cream
150ml/¼ pt thick natural yogurt

1. Melt the butter in a heavy-base frying pan and cook the almonds, stirring frequently, until golden brown. Stir in the sugar and cook, stirring, for about 1 minute or until the sugar dissolves and coats the almonds. Tip on to a baking tray lined with non-stick paper. Leave to cool.

2. Break the sponge fingers into a serving bowl (preferably glass). Combine the Madeira, brandy, orange rind and juice and sprinkle evenly over the sponge. Cover and leave to stand for about 30 minutes.

3. Whip the cream to soft peaks then fold in the yogurt. Spoon the mixture on top of the soaked sponge.

4. Chop the almonds roughly and scatter them over the top. Serve as soon as possible.

Syllabub

I am told that, hundreds of years ago syllabub (or sillabub) was created by dairy maids who would squirt warm milk, straight from the cow, into a vessel containing cider or sherry. These days we make syllabub with double cream and, as you will see, it is very easy to make. In this recipe you could, if you like, replace the orange juice with dry white wine, sherry or cider. Once made, it can be kept in the fridge for several hours before serving. Decorate with small strips of orange peel and serve with soft sponge fingers or crisp biscuits.

Serves 6

finely grated rind and juice of 1 lemon
juice of 1 orange
½ tsp ground cinnamon
70g/2½ oz caster sugar
300ml/½ pt double cream

1. In a bowl, put the lemon rind and juice and orange juice. Add the cinnamon and sugar and stir until dissolved.
2. Add the cream and whisk until the mixture is thick and creamy.
3. Pour into individual glasses and refrigerate until ready to serve.

Summer Pudding

Summer Pudding was originally developed to use up leftover bread. These days, it is a favourite (and fashionable) dessert. You need to make it the day before you want to serve it and the bread used should be a day old. When soft fruits are not in season, or when they are just too expensive, I use those packets of frozen fruits which are readily available in the supermarket freezers. To make Autumn Pudding, use a similar quantity of prepared autumn fruit, such as plums, blackberries, pears or apples, or a mixture. Serve it cold with cream or Greek-style yogurt.

Serves 4-6

675g/1½ lb mixed summer fruit, such as raspberries, strawberries, currants and cherries
55g/2 oz caster sugar or to taste
about 8 thin slices bread, crusts removed

1. Cook the fruit gently with 4 tbsp water, until soft (you can do this on the hob or in the microwave). Stir in sugar to taste.

2. From one slice of bread, cut a circle to fit the bottom of a 1.2 litre/2 pt pudding basin. Cut the remaining bread into fingers. Place the bread circle in the basin and line the sides with the fingers, overlapping them slightly and making sure there are not gaps.

3. Spoon the fruit mixture into the lined basin, reserving about 3 tbsp juice. Cover the fruit with bread.

4. Top with a plate or saucer that fits just inside the basin and put a weight on it (a can of food will do the job). Leave until cold then refrigerate overnight.

5. Remove the plate or saucer and carefully run a knife around the pudding to loosen it. Invert it on to a serving plate and spoon the reserved juice over the top.

Pancakes

Tradition has it that pancakes are served on the last day before Lent and they were originally developed to use up eggs and milk before fasting began. Shrove Tuesday, or Pancake Day, became a day of fun and games, with pancake races – often in fancy dress. If you like, add a little finely grated orange or lemon rind to the batter.

Makes about 10

115g/4 oz plain flour
pinch of salt
1 medium egg
300ml/½ pt milk
25g/1 oz melted butter, plus extra for brushing
sugar and lemon juice, to serve

1. Sift the flour and salt into a bowl. Made a well in the centre, add the egg and beat well, gradually adding the milk, to make a smooth batter. Stir in the 25g/1 oz melted butter.

2. Heat the pan (which should be about 18cm/7 in across and preferably non-stick). When hot, lightly brush the base with melted butter.

3. Into the hot pan, pour some batter, swirling in just enough to thinly coat the base of the pan. Cook for 1-2 minutes until golden brown. Turn the pancake over and cook the second side for about 1 minute until golden brown. Lift out and keep warm.

4. Repeat with the remaining batter.

5. Serve immediately, sprinkled with sugar and lemon juice.

Bread and Butter Pudding

A filling winter pudding which is usually a favourite with men. This recipe uses white bread, but you could use other varieties, including crusty French bread, fruit loaf, or sweet brioche. Instead of sultanas or raisins, try using chopped ready-to-eat dried apricots or dates, or some fresh fruit – thickly sliced bananas are luscious. Add a little vanilla or almond essence to the milk if you like. Do not be tempted to skip the standing time in step 3 – it allows the bread to soak up the liquid (and flavours) to make a light pudding.

Serves 4

6-8 large bread slices, about 1cm/½ in thick
50g/1¾ oz soft butter
50g/1¾ oz sultanas or raisins
40g/1½ oz caster sugar
2 medium eggs
600ml/1 pt milk or half milk and half double cream

1. Spread one side of each bread slice with butter. Cut each slice diagonally into four triangles.

2. Arrange half the bread, butter-side up, in a buttered 1.2 litre/2 pt ovenproof dish. Scatter the fruit over the top then sprinkle with half the sugar. Top with the remaining bread slices, buttered side up, and sprinkle the remaining sugar over.

3. Beat the eggs and stir in the milk. Strain the mixture and pour it evenly over the bread. Leave to stand for 30 minutes.

4. Cook in a preheated oven at 170°C/325°F/Gas 3 for ¾-1 hour until the bread is crisp and golden brown on the edges and the egg mixture is set in the centre.

Bakewell Pudding

The story told in Bakewell, Derbyshire, is about a cook at the local tavern who created a new recipe as the result of a mistake. Whether you believe it or not, Bakewell Tart (as it is often called) is a wonderful, buttery dessert or cake. It began as an oval puff pastry case with a thin layer of strawberry or raspberry jam beneath a sponge made with butter, sugar, eggs and ground almonds. Today, it's usually round and can be made with a plain or sweet shortcrust pastry. I often make it when I have some pastry leftover from another recipe. Serve it warm or cold with whipped cream, crème fraîche or custard.

Serves 6

175g/6 oz puff pastry, thawed if frozen
4 tbsp strawberry or raspberry jam
115g/4 oz ground almonds
115g/4 oz butter
85g/3 oz caster sugar
3 medium eggs, beaten
2-3 drops of almond essence

1. On a lightly floured surface, roll out the pastry and use to line an 18cm/7 in pie plate or flan tin.

2. Spread the jam over the bottom of the pastry case. Refrigerate it while you make the filling.

3. Put the almonds into a bowl and add the butter, sugar, eggs and essence. Beat well until smooth and light.

4. Spread the almond mixture evenly over the jam.

5. Cook in a preheated oven at 190°C/375°F/Gas 5 for about 30 minutes or until the surface is deep brown and firm to the touch.

Treacle Tart

A very sweet, open tart, with a filling of breadcrumbs and treacle and usually decorated with strips of pastry. Black treacle was probably used in the original recipe, but it was replaced by the more refined golden syrup after its development in the late 19th century. It would have been an economical dish. Serve it hot or cold with cream or custard.

Serves 6

225g/8 oz shortcrust pastry
75g/2¾ oz fresh breadcrumbs
½ tsp ground ginger
225g/8 oz golden syrup
finely grated rind and juice of 1 lemon
beaten egg (optional)

1. On a lightly floured surface, roll out the pastry and use to line a 20cm/8 in pie plate or flan dish. Reserve the pastry trimmings.

2. Mix the breadcrumbs and ginger and spread the mixture over the base of the pastry case.

3. In a pan on the hob (or in a bowl in the microwave), gently warm the syrup with the lemon rind and juice until runny. Pour evenly over the breadcrumbs.

4. Roll out the reserved pastry trimmings and cut into long thin strips. Lightly brush the edges of the tart with water. Arrange the strips in a lattice pattern on top of the tart, trimming the ends and pressing to seal the edges. If you wish, brush a little beaten egg over the pastry to glaze the edges and trimmings.

5. Cook in a preheated oven at 190°C/375°F/Gas 5 for about 25 minutes until the pastry is golden brown and the filling is set.

Butterscotch Tart

This dessert is a Scottish recipe, where it was likely to have been developed in the 17th century. It is quite sweet and comprises a pastry case with a butterscotch filling which is topped with meringue. Serve it warm or cold with cream or thick natural yogurt.

Serves 4-6

175g/6 oz shortcrust pastry
150g/5½ oz soft brown sugar
50g/1¾ oz plain flour
200ml/7 fl oz milk
50g/1¾ oz butter
½ tsp vanilla extract
1 large egg, separated
50g/1¾ oz caster sugar

1. On a lightly floured surface, roll out the pastry and use to line a 20cm/8 in ovenproof flan dish.

2. Line the pastry case with a circle of baking or greaseproof paper and half-fill with baking beans, dried beans or rice. Cook in a preheated oven at 190°C/375°F/Gas 5 for 15 minutes. Remove the beans and paper.

3. Put the brown sugar into a pan and sift the flour over. Whisk in the milk, then add the butter. Cook over medium heat, stirring continuously with the whisk, until the mixture comes to the boil and is thick. Remove from the heat and beat in the vanilla extract and the egg yolk.

4. In a clean bowl, whisk the egg white until stiff peaks are formed. With a metal spoon, fold in the caster sugar.

5. Pour the butterscotch mixture into the pastry case and level the top. Spread the meringue evenly over the top.

6. Cook in a preheated oven at 150°C/300°F/Gas 2 for 20-30 minutes until the meringue is crisp and golden brown.

Christmas Pudding

It was in Victorian days that plum pudding became the traditional end to the Christmas meal. During the making of the pudding it was, and still is, traditional for family members to take turns in stirring the mixture (clockwise only) and, at the same time, making a wish. In addition, lucky charms or silver coins would be buried in the pudding. I still remember the excitement, as a child, of finding a silver sixpence in my pudding bowl.

I'm not ashamed to tell you that a close friend of mine, June Ellis, makes my Christmas pudding every year – and it's the best I have ever tasted. This recipe is based on the one she uses. For the best flavour, make it in November then let it mature until Christmas. Serve it with a sweet white sauce or brandy butter.

Serves 8-10

55g/2 oz plain flour
1 tsp ground mixed spice
115g/4 oz fresh breadcrumbs
140g/5 oz shredded suet
115g/4 oz soft dark brown sugar
400g/14 oz mixed dried fruit
55g/2 oz blanched almonds, roughly chopped
1 small carrot, finely grated
grated rind of 1 small orange
2 medium eggs, beaten
2 tbsp brandy or dry sherry
1 tsp almond essence
75ml/2½ fl oz milk

1. Into a large bowl, sift the flour and spice. Mix in the breadcrumbs, suet, sugar, fruit, nuts, carrot and orange rind. Add the eggs, brandy, essence and milk. Mix well.

2. Spoon the mixture into a buttered 1.2 litre/2 pt pudding basin and level the top. Cover with buttered greaseproof, baking paper or foil, making a pleat to allow the pudding to rise. Secure with string around the top of the basin and make a string handle (for easy removal from the pan).

3. Put in a steamer over boiling water. Alternatively, put on to a trivet in a large saucepan with boiling water to come half way up the sides of the basin.

4. Cover and steam (allowing the water to bubble only gently) for about 6 hours, topping up with boiling water as needed.

5. Lift the pudding out and leave to stand until cold.

6. Cover securely with foil and store in a cool place.

7. To serve, steam as above for 2 hours. Alternatively, remove foil and cover securely with greaseproof or baking paper and microwave on MED-LOW for about 15 minutes or until hot throughout.

8. Turn out on to a warmed serving dish.

Syrup Sponge Pudding

This pudding became very popular in the late 1800s when golden syrup made an appearance. Since then, it has become a favourite in all parts of the country. However, our changing lifestyles have resulted in less time to spend in the kitchen watching over a steaming pot. Below, I have included the traditional method, but it is so much more convenient to cook it in the microwave. The syrup can be replaced with any kind of jam, with marmalade, mincemeat or lemon curd. The sponge mixture can be flavoured with finely grated lemon or orange rind. To make a chocolate pudding, omit the syrup, blend 4 tbsp cocoa powder with 1 tbsp hot water and stir into the beaten butter and sugar in step 2. Serve with custard.

Serves 4-6

3 tbsp golden syrup
115g/4 oz soft butter
115g/4 oz caster sugar
2 medium eggs, lightly beaten
few drops of vanilla essence
175g/6 oz self-raising flour, sifted
2 tbsp milk

1. Butter a 1.2 litre/2 pt pudding basin and spoon the syrup into the bottom.

2. In a large bowl, beat the butter and sugar together until light and fluffy. Gradually beat in the eggs and vanilla essence then, using a metal spoon, fold in the sifted flour and the milk.

3. Spoon the mixture on top of the syrup and level the top.

4. Cover with buttered greaseproof, baking paper or foil, making a pleat to allow the pudding to rise. Secure with string around the top of the basin and make a string handle (for easy removal from the pan).

5. Put in a steamer over boiling water. Alternatively, put on to a trivet in a large saucepan with boiling water to come half way up the sides of the basin.

6. Cover and steam (allowing the water to bubble only gently) for about 1½ hours, topping up with boiling water as needed.

7. Lift the pudding out and turn out on to a warm serving plate.

To microwave:

1. Butter a 1.2 litre/2 pt pudding basin and spoon the syrup into the bottom.

2. In a large bowl, beat the butter and sugar together until light and fluffy. Gradually beat in the eggs and vanilla essence then, using a metal spoon, fold in the sifted flour and the milk.

3. Spoon the mixture on top of the syrup and level the top.

4. Cover loosely with a 'hat' of buttered greaseproof or baking paper.

5. Cook on MED-HIGH for 6-8 minutes or until the surface of the pudding is still slightly moist while the mixture beneath it is cooked.

6. Leave to stand for 5 minutes before turning out on to a warm serving plate.

Queen of Puddings

Another 'old fashioned' favourite which has become popular on pub menus. Mrs Beeton called this 'Queen of Bread Puddings'. A layer of breadcrumbs, flavoured with lemon rind, is spread with sweet jam and topped with golden meringue. Serve it just as it is or with cream or with a fruit purée.

Serves 4

115g/4 oz fresh white breadcrumbs
115g/4 oz caster sugar
finely grated rind of 1 small lemon
425ml/¾ pt milk
25g/1 oz butter
2 medium eggs, separated
2 tbsp raspberry jam

1. In a large bowl, mix together the breadcrumbs, 25g/1 oz sugar and the lemon rind.

2. Put the milk and butter into a pan and heat gently until the butter has melted. Pour over the breadcrumb mixture and leave to stand for 30 minutes.

3. Add the egg yolks to the cooled breadcrumb mixture and mix well. Spoon into a buttered 850ml/1½ pt ovenproof dish.

4. Cook in a preheated oven at 170°/325°F/Gas 3 for about 30 minutes or until set.

5. Drop small spoonfuls of the jam over the hot surface of the pudding.

6. In a clean bowl, whisk the egg whites until stiff. Using a metal spoon, fold in the remaining 85g/3 oz sugar. Spoon the meringue over the top of the pudding.

7. Continue cooking at 170°/325°F/Gas 3 for about 30 minutes or until the meringue is set and golden brown.

To microwave:

1. In a large bowl, mix together the breadcrumbs, 25g/1 oz sugar and the lemon rind.

2. Heat the milk and butter on HIGH for about 2 minutes or until the butter has melted. Pour over the breadcrumb mixture and leave to stand for 30 minutes.

3. Add the egg yolks to the cooled breadcrumb mixture and mix well. Spoon into a buttered 850ml/1½ pt ovenproof dish.

4. Cook, uncovered, on MEDIUM for about 8 minutes or until just set.

5. Drop small spoonfuls of the jam over the hot surface of the pudding.

6. In a clean bowl, whisk the egg whites until stiff. Using a metal spoon, fold in the remaining 85g/3 oz sugar. Spoon the meringue over the top of the pudding

7. Cook, uncovered, on MEDIUM for 3-4 minutes until the meringue is risen and set. If you like, lightly brown the top of the pudding under a medium-hot grill.

Clootie Dumpling

This Scottish dessert, a dumpling traditionally boiled in a cloth, is served at Hogmanay or New Year. The first visitors after midnight (first footers) are offered a piece of Clootie Dumpling with a tot of whisky. A Scottish friend of mine always looks forward to visiting her old home – each time she does, her mother makes a pudding. To prepare it authentically, the dumpling should be cooked in a floured cloth, tied loosely to allow it to expand. I like to make mine in a pudding basin. Serve it with a custard or fruit sauce or cold, sliced and sprinkled with caster sugar or lightly fried in butter.

Serves 4-6

85g/3 oz self-raising flour
1 tsp baking powder, 1 tsp ground cinnamon, 1 tsp ground nutmeg
85g/3 oz fresh white breadcrumbs
85g/3 oz caster sugar
85g/3 oz shredded suet
175g/6 oz mixed dried fruit
1 crisp eating apple, such as Cox's, peeled and grated
1 small carrot, finely grated
1 tbsp black treacle
1 medium egg, lightly beaten
finely grated rind of 1 orange
about 150ml/¼ pt milk

1. Into a large bowl, sift the flour, baking powder and spices. Stir in the remaining ingredients and mix well, adding sufficient milk to make a soft (but quite stiff) consistency. Spoon the mixture into a buttered 1.2 litre/2 pt pudding basin.
2. Cover with buttered greaseproof, baking paper or foil, making a pleat to allow the pudding to rise. Secure with string around the top of the basin and make a string handle (for easy removal from the pan).
3. Put in a steamer over boiling water. Alternatively, put on to a trivet in a large saucepan with boiling water to come half way up the sides of the basin.
4. Cover and steam (allowing the water to bubble only gently) for 2-2½ hours, topping up with boiling water as needed, until the pudding is well risen and firm to the touch.
5. Lift out, remove cover and carefully turn out on to a warm plate.

Baked Egg Custard

A creamy custard baked in the oven. In the 19th century, the custard may well have been flavoured with bay leaves, cinnamon or lemon. Today, we are likely to use a vanilla pod (heated with the liquid in step 1) or vanilla extract. Many recipes use milk but the recipe below includes single cream to make a rich treat. If you have a particularly sweet tooth, add a little more sugar (up to 25g/1 oz extra only). Serve it warm or chilled, just as it is or with some fresh soft fruit, such as raspberries or strawberries.

Serves 4-6

600ml single cream or full-cream milk
3 medium eggs, beaten
25g/1 oz caster sugar
1 tsp vanilla extract
freshly grated nutmeg

1. Heat the cream or milk gently, but do not allow it to boil.

2. Meanwhile, beat the eggs with the sugar. Lightly butter an 850ml/1½ pt pie or soufflé dish.

3. Pour the hot cream or milk on to the egg, whisking continuously. Stir in the vanilla extract.

4. Strain the custard into the prepared dish and sprinkle the top with nutmeg.

5. Stand the dish in a roasting tin or dish containing sufficient hot water to come half way up the sides of the dish.

6. Cook at 170°C/325°F/Gas 3 for about ¾-1 hour until the custard is set.

To microwave:

1. Complete steps 1-4.

2. Stand the dish in a large (microwaveable) container with sufficient boiling water (from the kettle) to come half way up the sides of the dish.

3. Cook on MED-LOW for about 20 minutes or until just set.

Upside Down Pudding with Pears

The idea for this pudding was probably developed in Victorian times. It is easy to make, yet it looks impressive. Make it with fresh ripe fruit or with canned fruit. Try apricot, peach, plum or pear halves; pineapple rings; trimmed short lengths of rhubarb; or peeled, cored and sliced apples. Use brown or white sugar; add spices (ground ginger, cinnamon or mixed spice) to the cake mixture. To make a chocolate version, replace 25g/1 oz flour with the same quantity of cocoa powder. Serve the pudding hot with cream, thick yogurt or custard.

Serves 6

175g/6 oz butter
50g/1¾ oz soft brown sugar
3 glacé cherries, halved
3 ripe pears, peeled, halved and cores removed
115g/4 oz caster sugar
3 medium eggs, lightly beaten
175g/6 oz self-raising flour
3 tbsp milk

1. Melt 55g/2 oz butter on the hob and pour it into a 20cm/8 in cake tin, tipping it so that the butter coats the base. Sprinkle the brown sugar evenly over the butter.

2. Place a cherry half into the cavity of each pear half. Arrange the pears, cut side down and tops to the centre, in the tin.

3. In a mixing bowl, beat the remaining butter with the caster sugar until light and fluffy. Gradually beat in the eggs. Sift the flour over the top and, with a metal spoon, fold in with the milk.

4. Carefully spread the cake mixture over the pears.

5. Cook in a preheated oven at 180°C/350°F/Gas 4 for about 45 minutes or until risen and firm to the touch.

6. Leave to stand for about 5 minutes before loosening the sides and turning out on to a warmed serving plate.

To microwave:

1. Melt 55g/2 oz butter in the microwave and pour it into a 20cm/8 in soufflé dish, tipping it so that the butter coats the base. Sprinkle the brown sugar evenly over the butter.

2. Place a cherry half into the cavity of each pear half. Arrange the pears, cut side down and tops to the centre, in the tin.

3. In a mixing bowl, beat the remaining butter with the caster sugar until light and fluffy. Gradually beat in the eggs. Sift the flour over the top and, with a metal spoon, fold in with the milk.

4. Carefully spread the cake mixture over the pears.

5. Cook on **MED-HIGH** for about 6 minutes or until the surface is still slightly moist and the cake underneath it is cooked through (a skewer inserted in the centre should come out clean).

6. Leave to stand for about 5 minutes before loosening the sides and turning out on to a warmed serving plate.

Pond Pudding

Sussex is the county which is usually associated with Pond Pudding. A whole lemon is cooked with butter and sugar inside suet-crust pastry. On cutting into the pudding, a bright pool of buttery sauce flows out. You will need a sharp knife to cut the lemon so that everyone is served a piece of it. Serve it with cream or thick natural yogurt.

Serves 4-6

225g/8 oz self-raising flour
115g/4 oz shredded suet
140g/5 oz butter, cut into small cubes
140g/5 oz light soft brown sugar
1 large lemon, well washed

1. Butter a 1.2 litre/2pt pudding basin.

2. Sift the flour into a bowl and mix in the suet. Stir in about 150ml/¼ pt cold water or sufficient to make a soft dough. Roll out two thirds of the dough and use to line the prepared basin.

3. Put half the butter cubes and half the sugar into the basin. Prick the lemon all over with a thin skewer. Gently press the lemon into the centre of the butter and sugar mixture. Pack the remaining butter cubes and sugar around the lemon.

4. Roll out the remaining dough to make a lid. Wet the edges with water and press on to the basin, sealing the edges well. Cover with a double thickness of buttered greaseproof or baking paper (make a large pleat in it to allow the pudding to rise) and tie on securely.

5. Steam for 3 hours, either in a steamer or a trivet in a large saucepan with gently boiling water to come half way up the sides of the basin (check frequently, topping up with extra boiling water as necessary).

5

CAKES & BAKES

There is nothing more welcoming or mouth watering than the aroma that wafts out to greet you from a kitchen where baking is going on. For me, the recipes in this section are reminiscent of times when it was normal to have 'baking days'. At least one of them is bound to be a favourite of yours.

Yorkshire Curd Tarts

These rich tarts were traditionally served on sheep farms at shearing time. Originally the filling would probably have been quite plain, before the recipe developed to include dried fruit. Don't be tempted to leave out the alcohol – it makes all the difference to the finished flavour. Serve these tarts, which are sometimes called Maids of Honour, warm or cold.

Makes about 24

Pastry:
225g/8 oz plain flour
115g/4 oz butter or block margarine, diced
25g/1 oz caster sugar
1 egg, lightly beaten

Filling:
225g/8 oz curd cheese
115g/4 oz caster sugar
55g/2 oz butter or block margarine, melted
55g/2 oz currants
2 eggs, lightly beaten
finely grated rind of 1 lemon
good pinch of freshly grated nutmeg
1 tbsp brandy or rum

1. To make the pastry, sift the flour into a large bowl and add the butter. Using your fingertips, rub the butter into the flour until the mixture resembles fine breadcrumbs (this can be done in a processor). Stir in the sugar, then add the egg, stirring until the mixture begins to cling together. Gather up the mixture to make a firm dough. Wrap and chill for about 30 minutes to allow the pastry to 'relax'.

2. Roll out the pastry and use to line 24 lightly-greased patty tins.

3. To make the filling, beat the curd cheese with the sugar until smooth. Stir in the remaining ingredients and beat until well mixed.

4. Spoon the filling into the pastry cases.

5. Put into a preheated oven and cook at 180°C/350°F/Gas 4 for about 25 minutes or until set and golden brown.

Apple Cake

There are many versions of Apple Cake, depending on whether you are close to the apple orchards of the West Country or of Kent. Here is just one which I make often. Serve it warm with cream as a dessert, or cold as a cake.

Makes about 12 slices

175g/6 oz butter, softened
175g/6 oz dark soft brown sugar
3 medium eggs, lightly beaten
225g/8 oz self-raising flour
1½ tsp ground mixed spice
450g/1 lb Bramley apples, peeled, cored and finely chopped
2-3 tbsp apple juice or milk
sugar for dusting

1. Grease and line a 20cm/8 in round cake tin with baking paper.

2. Beat the butter and sugar until light and creamy. Beat in the eggs, a little at a time. Sift in the flour and spice and mix well. Fold in the apples and sufficient apple juice to make a soft dropping consistency. Spoon the mixture into the prepared tin and level the top.

3. Put into a preheated oven and cook at 180°/350°F/Gas 4 for about 1¼ hours or until golden brown and firm to the touch.

4. Leave in the tin for 15 minutes before carefully turning out and cooling on a wire rack. Dust with sugar before serving.

Cornish Saffron Cake

A traditional cake which is to be found in most bakeries in Cornwall. Its beautiful colour is due to the addition of saffron. One of the world's most expensive spices, saffron is made from the dried stigmas of the purple-flowering saffron crocus, which originates from Saffron Walden in Essex. I like to use saffron strands (they look pretty speckled through the cake) but you can use powder. Yeast is the raising agent and it is this that gives the cake its bread-like texture. Since fresh yeast can be difficult to obtain these days, I use dried. Serve the cake sliced and spread with butter.

Makes about 18 slices

pinch of saffron strands
150ml/¼ pt milk
1 tsp sugar
2 tsp easy-bake or easy-blend dried yeast
450g/1 lb plain flour, plus extra for kneading
½ tsp salt
85g/3 oz butter, diced
55g/2 oz lard, diced
55g/2 oz caster sugar
55g/2 oz currants
55g/2 oz sultanas
55g/2 oz mixed peel, finely chopped
beaten egg

1. Put the saffron in a bowl, add 150ml/¼ pt boiling water, cover and leave to stand for several hours or overnight for the colour to develop.

2. Mix together the saffron and its liquid, milk, sugar and yeast. Leave to stand for about 15 minutes or until frothy.

3. Meanwhile, sieve the flour and salt into a large bowl. Rub in the butter and lard until the mixture resembles fine breadcrumbs. Stir in the sugar, currants, sultanas and peel.

4. Make a well in the centre and add the yeast liquid. Mix to a soft smooth dough (do not worry if it is a little sticky). Cover with oiled film and put in a warm place until doubled in size (about 1 hour).

5. Meanwhile, grease and line a 900g/2 lb loaf tin with baking paper.

6. Turn the dough on to a lightly floured surface and knock the air out, kneading until smooth. Put into the prepared tin, cover with oiled film and leave in a warm place to rise for about 30 minutes.

7. Lightly brush the top with beaten egg. Put into a preheated oven and cook at 200°C/400°F/Gas 6 for about 45 minutes or until risen and firm to the touch (a fine skewer inserted in the centre should come out clean). If it starts to become too brown, cover the top with a sheet of foil. Leave to cool in the tin for about 20 minutes, then turn out on to a wire rack to cool completely.

Bara Brith

Bara Brith is Welsh for 'speckled bread'. It is usually served sliced and spread with butter. The original version would probably have been made using left-over bread dough then, later on, a special recipe was created. More recently, quick-to-make versions were developed, using self raising flour and egg to produce a more cake-like result. Because I am Welsh, I feel duty-bound to include a recipe for each!

Makes 1 large loaf

WITH YEAST:

225g/8 oz mixed dried fruit and chopped peel
350ml/12 fl oz hot strong tea, strained
450g/1 lb strong white flour
50g/1¾ oz soft brown sugar
1 tsp salt
½ tsp ground mixed spice
7g sachet easy-bake or easy-blend yeast
50g/1¾ oz butter, melted
milk, to mix if necessary

1. Put the fruit into a heatproof dish and pour in the hot tea. Cover and leave to soak at room temperature for several hours or overnight.

2. Into a large warmed bowl, sieve the flour, sugar, salt and spice. Stir in the yeast.

3. Add the fruit and its liquid and the melted butter. Stir to make a soft smooth dough, adding a little milk if necessary, then use your hands to mix well and stretch the dough until it becomes elastic. Cover with oiled film and leave in a warm place for about 1½ hours or until the dough has doubled its size.

4. Meanwhile, grease and line a 900g/2 lb loaf tin with baking paper.

5. Turn the dough on to a lightly floured surface, knocking the excess air out, and then shape it into a loaf. Put, seam-side down, into the prepared tin. Cover with oiled film and leave in a warm place for about 1½ hours until the loaf has doubled its size.

6. Put into a preheated oven and cook at 200°C/400°F/Gas 6 for about 40 minutes until well risen, golden brown and cooked through (when removed from the tin and the underneath is tapped, it should sound hollow). Turn out and leave to cool completely on a wire rack.

WITH SELF RAISING FLOUR:

225g/8 oz mixed dried fruit and chopped peel
225ml/8 fl oz hot strong tea, strained
225g/8 oz self raising flour
1 tsp ground mixed spice
25g/1 oz butter
100g/3¾ oz soft brown sugar
1 medium egg, lightly beaten

1. Put the fruit into a heatproof dish and pour in the hot tea. Cover and leave to soak at room temperature for several hours or overnight.

2. Grease and line a 900g/2 lb loaf tin with baking paper.

3. Into a large bowl, sieve the flour and spice. Rub in the butter until the mixture resembles fine breadcrumbs. Stir in the sugar. Add the fruit and its liquid and the egg. Mix well.

4. Pour the mixture into the prepared loaf tin. Cook in a preheated oven at 180°C/350°F/Gas 4 for about 1 hour or until a skewer inserted in the centre comes out clean.

5. Turn out on a wire rack and leave to cool completely.

Welsh Cakes

Not so many years ago, Welsh Cakes would be cooked at least once a week in most households in Wales. They are still served as a traditional welcome to visitors. Make them on a griddle or bakestone or use a heavy-base (preferably non-stick) frying pan. Serve them warm or cold.

Makes about 15

225g/8 oz plain flour
1 tsp baking powder
pinch of salt
115g/4 oz butter or a mixture of butter and lard, diced
85g/3 oz caster sugar
70g/2½ oz currants
1 egg, lightly beaten
about 2 tbsp milk
caster sugar for dusting

1. Sift the flour, baking powder and salt into a large bowl. Rub in the butter until the mixture resembles fine breadcrumbs (this can be done in a processor). Stir in the sugar and currants. Add the egg and mix, adding sufficient milk to make a soft dough which comes away from the sides of the bowl. It should be quite smooth.

2. On a lightly floured surface, roll out the dough to about 5mm/¼ in thick. With a 6-7.5 cm/2½-3 in cutter, cut into rounds. Gather up the scraps, roll out again and cut into rounds.

3. Cook on a preheated lightly-greased griddle, bakestone or heavy-base pan for about 5 minutes on each side or until risen, set and golden brown.

4. Lift on to a wire rack, dust with sugar and leave to cool.

Dundee Cake

Scottish ports such as Dundee used to be famous centres for the import and distribution of spices, fruits and nuts. This traditional recipe marries all three ingredients.

Serves about 16

300g/10½ oz plain flour
1 tbsp ground mixed spice
225g/8 oz butter, softened
225g/8 oz caster sugar
finely grated rind of 1 large orange
5 medium eggs
175g/6 oz currants
175g/6 oz raisins
175g/6 oz sultanas
55g/2 oz glacé cherries, quartered
115g/4 oz mixed peel, finely chopped
55g/2 oz whole blanched almonds

1. Grease and line a 20cm/8 in round cake tin with baking paper.

2. Sift the flour and spice and set aside.

3. In a large bowl, beat the butter, sugar and orange rind until light and creamy. Beat in the eggs, one at a time, adding a little of the flour with each.

4. Fold in the remaining flour. Stir in the currants and raisins. Add the sultanas, cherries and peel and stir in.

5. Spoon the mixture into the prepared tin and level the top. Arrange the almonds on top.

6. Put into a preheated oven and cook at 170°C/325°F/Gas 3 for about 2-2½ hours. If the top starts to become too brown, cover it with a disc of baking paper or foil. The cake is cooked when a metal skewer inserted in the centre comes out clean. Leave in the tin for 20 minutes, then carefully turn it out, remove all paper and cool completely on a wire rack.

Simnel Cake

This cake is traditionally served on Easter Sunday, when the marzipan balls on top represent the eleven faithful apostles, with Judas excluded. It is also associated with Mothering Sunday, when the plain marzipan topping is usually decorated with tiny spring flowers – either fresh or crystallised.

Serves 16

225g/8 oz butter, softened
225g/8 oz caster sugar
finely grated rind of 1 orange
5 medium eggs
300g/10½ oz plain flour, sieved
1 tbsp mixed spice
225g/8 oz currants, 225g/8 oz sultanas, 225g/8 oz raisins
50g/1¾ oz glacé cherries, roughly chopped
115g/4 oz dried mixed peel
1-2 tbsp milk
450g/1 lb marzipan

1. Grease and line the base of a 20cm/8 in round cake tin with baking paper.
2. In a large bowl, beat the butter, sugar and orange rind until light and creamy. Beat in the eggs, one at a time, adding a little of the flour with each. Fold in the remaining flour and the spice. Gently stir in the fruit, adding sufficient milk to make a soft consistency.
3. Spoon half the mixture into the prepared tin and level the surface.
4. Roll out one third of the marzipan to make a 20cm/8 in circle. Place on top of the mixture in the tin.
5. Spoon the remaining cake mixture on top and level the surface.
6. Cook in a preheated oven at 150°C/300°F/Gas 2 for about 3 hours or until a fine skewer inserted in the centre shows traces of marzipan only, and not uncooked cake mixture.
7. Leave in the tin for at least 30 minutes before carefully turning out to cool completely on a wire rack.
8. Roll out half of the remaining marzipan to make a 20cm/8 in circle. Press on top of the cake. Shape the last piece of marzipan into 11 balls and arrange them around the edge of the cake, pressing them down lightly. If wished, grill the marzipan top until light golden brown.

Scotch Pancakes

Traditionally cooked on a griddle or bakestone, Scotch Pancakes can also be cooked in a heavy-base (preferably non-stick) frying pan. They are best eaten warm, soon after they have been cooked, with butter, golden syrup or honey. Earlier recipes would have used plain flour with raising agents (bicarbonate of soda and cream of tartar). These days, I use self-raising flour. The mixture should be cooked as soon as it is made, so have the griddle hot and ready.

Makes 10-15

115g/4 oz self-raising flour
2 tbsp caster sugar
1 medium egg, lightly beaten
about 150ml/¼ pt milk

1. Preheat and lightly grease a griddle, bakestone or heavy-base frying pan.

2. Sift the flour and mix with the sugar. Make a well in the centre and add the egg. Stir, gradually adding sufficient milk to make a thick creamy batter.

3. Drop spoonfuls of the mixture on to the hot surface of the griddle or pan. Cook for 2-3 minutes or until bubbles rise to, and burst on, the surface of the pancakes. Turn the pancakes over (a palette knife is good for doing this) and cook for a further 2-3 minutes.

4. Keep the cooked pancakes warm while you cook the remaining mixture.

Gingerbread

Gingerbread has always been popular in the north of England and in Scotland, where there exists a variety of recipes. To enjoy this one at its best, keep the gingerbread for 2-3 days in an airtight container or wrapped in foil, before cutting and serving.

Makes about 9 squares

350g/12 oz plain flour
½ tsp salt
1 tbsp ground ginger
2 tsp baking powder
½ tsp bicarbonate of soda
175g/6 oz dark soft brown sugar
115g/4 oz butter
225g/8 oz golden syrup
1 medium egg, lightly beaten
200ml/7 fl oz milk

1. Grease and line a 20cm/8 in square cake tin with baking paper.

2. Into a mixing bowl, sift the flour, salt, ginger, baking powder and bicarbonate of soda.

3. Put the sugar, butter and syrup into a small pan and heat gently, stirring occasionally, until just melted. (Alternatively, put the ingredients in a heatproof bowl or jug and heat in the microwave.) Remove from the heat.

4. Whisk the egg into the milk. Add the milk and syrup mixtures to the flour and beat well until smooth. Pour into the prepared tin.

5. Put into a preheated oven and cook at 180°C/350°F/Gas 4 for about 50 minutes or until firm to the touch and golden brown.

6. Turn out and cool on a wire rack. To serve, cut into squares (see note above).

Oatmeal Parkin

This cake has various names, usually associated with the area from which it comes – Yorkshire Parkin, Lancashire Parkin. Traditionally it is served on Bonfire or Guy Fawkes' Night. Resist the temptation to eat it immediately after cooking – it tastes even nicer after being stored in an airtight container or wrapped in foil for 3-4 days.

Makes about 9 squares

225g/8 oz plain flour
2 tsp ground ginger
1 tsp mixed spice
2 tsp bicarbonate of soda
175g/6 oz fine or medium oatmeal
225g/8 oz black treacle
115g/4 oz butter
115g/4 oz soft brown sugar
2 medium eggs, beaten
150ml/¼ pt milk

1. Grease and line a 20cm/8 in square cake tin with baking paper.

2. Into a mixing bowl, sift the flour, spices and bicarbonate of soda. Stir in the oatmeal.

3. Put the treacle, butter and sugar into a small pan and heat gently, stirring occasionally, until the butter just melted. (Alternatively, put the ingredients in a heatproof bowl or jug and heat in the microwave.) Remove from the heat and stir until smooth.

4. Whisk the eggs into the milk. Add the milk and treacle mixtures to the bowl and beat well until smooth. Pour into the prepared tin.

5. Put into a preheated oven and cook at 180°C/350°F/Gas 4 for about 45 minutes or until firm to the touch.

6. Turn out and cool on a wire rack (see note about storing, above).

Seed Cake

This buttery cake carries the distinctive flavour of caraway seeds. In the 17th and 18th centuries, caraway seeds were an everyday ingredient in baking. These days, sadly, they are hardly used at all – a great shame, since they give out a wonderful perfume. Originally, seed cake would have been made in a 15cm/6 in tin, but it's so good that I make a larger one.

Makes about 12 slices

175g/6 oz soft butter
175g/6 oz caster sugar
3 medium eggs, beaten
250g/9 oz self-raising flour, sifted
40g/1½ oz chopped mixed peel
1 tbsp caraway seeds
2 tbsp milk

1. Lightly butter a 20cm/8 in round cake tin and line it with baking paper.

2. In a mixing bowl, beat the butter and sugar until light and fluffy. Beat in the eggs, a little at a time. Using a metal spoon, fold in the flour, peel, seeds and milk.

3. Spoon the mixture into the prepared tin and level the surface.

4. Cook in a preheated oven at 180°C/350°F/Gas 4 for about 1 hour or until a skewer inserted in the centre comes out clean.

5. Leave in the tin for 10-15 minutes then turn out on to a wire rack and leave to cool completely.

Bread Pudding

There have been recipes for bread pudding ever since the 1700s. It makes wonderfully rich, filling, spicy, winter fare and is an excellent way of using up stale bread. Cooking it in an ovenproof loaf dish rather than a metal tin guarantees a moist result. Serve it warm with custard or cream, or cold as a cake, just as it is (with a cup of tea or coffee). It will keep for several days in a sealed tin or wrapped in foil.

Serves 8

225g/8 oz stale bread, weighed after removing crusts
300ml/½ pt milk
50g/1¾ oz dark brown sugar
85g/3 oz shredded suet or chilled grated butter
85g/3 oz currants
85g/3 oz sultanas
50g/1¾ oz chopped mixed peel
1 tbsp mixed spice
finely grated rind of 1 small orange
finely grated rind of 1 small lemon
1 medium egg, lightly beaten
whole nutmeg or grated nutmeg
caster sugar

1. Break the bread into small pieces, put into a large mixing bowl and pour the milk over. Leave to soak for 30 minutes.

2. Meanwhile, butter a large (900g/2 lb) ovenproof loaf dish.

3. Using a fork, gently break up the bread. Stir in the sugar, suet, fruit, peel, spice and orange and lemon rind. Beat in the egg, adding a little juice from the orange and/or lemon if necessary, to make a very soft dropping consistency.

4. Pour the mixture into the prepared dish, level the surface and finely grate some nutmeg over the top.

5. Cook in a preheated oven at 180°C/350°F/Gas 4 for about 1¼-1½ hours or until brown on top and firm to the touch.

6. Sprinkle some caster sugar over the top and leave to cool.

Half Pound Cake

As its name suggests, most of the ingredients are added in half-pound quantities – it's a recipe that is easy to memorise.

Makes about 16 slices

225g/8 oz butter, softened
225g/8 oz caster sugar
4 medium eggs, beaten
225g/8 oz plain flour, sifted
225g/8 oz raisins
225g/8 oz mixed sultanas and currants
115g/4 oz glacé cherries, halved
½ tsp ground mixed spice
1 tbsp brandy or sherry
pinch of salt

1. Grease and line a deep 20cm/8 in round cake tin with baking paper.

2. In a large bowl, beat the butter and sugar until light and creamy. Gradually beat in the eggs. Fold in the remaining ingredients.

3. Spoon into the prepared tin and level the top.

4. Cook in a preheated oven at 150°C/300°F/Gas 2 for 2-2½ hours or until firm to the touch and a skewer inserted in the centre comes out clean. If the top starts to get too brown, cover with baking paper.

5. Leave to cool in the tin for about 30 minutes, then turn out and cool completely on a wire rack.

Vinegar Cake

During the Second World War, the shortage of eggs prompted the creation of this cake. The cake rises with the help of bicarbonate of soda and vinegar instead of eggs. The finished cake doesn't taste at all vinegary – in fact it's lovely. Malt vinegar is used in this standard recipe, but you could use cider, wine or sherry vinegar. Like many fruit cakes, it is delicious served with cheese.

Makes about 16 slices

450g/1 lb plain flour
225g/8 oz butter, cut into cubes
225g/8 oz soft brown sugar
450g/1 lb mixed dried fruit
1 tsp bicarbonate of soda
300ml/½ pt milk
3 tbsp malt vinegar

1. Grease and line the base of a 23cm/9 in round cake tin with baking paper.

2. Sift the flour into a large bowl, then rub in the butter until the mixture resembles fine breadcrumbs (this can be done in a processor). Stir in the sugar and fruit.

3. Sprinkle the bicarbonate of soda into the milk and add the vinegar. As it froths up, stir the mixture into the dry ingredients.

4. Spoon into the prepared tin and level the top.

5. Cook in a preheated oven at 200°C/400°F/Gas 6 for 20-30 minutes, then continue on 170°/325°/Gas 3 for a further 1-1½ hours or until firm to the touch and a skewer inserted in the centre comes out clean. If the top starts to get too brown, cover it with baking paper.

6. Leave to cool in the tin for about 30 minutes, then turn out and cool completely on a wire rack.

Singing Hinnies

The north-east of England is famous for its Singing Hinnies. Singing refers to the noise they make during cooking as they sizzle on the hot griddle. Hinny is a term of affection – 'honey'. In the 1800s they were a favourite at children's birthday parties and often contained lucky charms. If you do not have a griddle, use a heavy-based frying pan – preferably non-stick. Serve them hot, split and buttered.

Makes about 20

350g/12 oz self raising flour
50g/1¾ oz ground rice
2 tsp baking powder
1 tsp salt
50g/1¾ oz caster sugar
50g/1¾ oz lard
85g/3 oz currants
about 150ml/¼ pt milk

1. Into a large bowl, sift the flour, rice, baking powder and salt. Add the sugar. Using your fingertips, rub in the lard until the mixture resembles coarse crumbs. Stir in the currants. Add the milk, stirring to make a soft dough.

2. On a lightly floured surface, roll out the dough into a circle about 5mm/¼ in thick. With a 6cm/2½ in cutter, cut into rounds, gathering up the off cuts and rolling out again.

3. Cook on a preheated lightly-greased griddle or bakestone for 3-4 minutes on each side until browned, risen and set.

Oatcakes

Wales and the Midlands have recipes for oatcakes, but it is the traditional Scottish variety which is the best known. Their flavour is best appreciated when they are served, either warm or cold, with cheese. If you like them slightly sweet, add a couple of teaspoons of caster sugar in step 1.

Makes about 12

115g/4 oz fine oatmeal, plus extra for rolling
¼ tsp baking powder
pinch of salt
15g/½ butter or lard

1. Put the oatmeal, baking powder and salt into a large bowl.
2. Put the butter or lard into 150ml/¼ pt water and heat until the fat has melted (do this on the hob or in the microwave). Stir enough of the liquid into the dry ingredients to make a firm dough.
3. On a surface lightly dusted with oatmeal, roll out the dough to about 3mm/⅛ in thick. With a 7.5cm/3 in cutter, cut into rounds, re-rolling the dough as necessary (alternatively, cut into triangles). Arrange on a baking sheet.
4. Cook in a preheated oven at 180°C/350°F/Gas 4 for about 25 minutes or until crisp and pale golden.

Scones

Scones are a favourite tea-time treat all over the country. Make them plain, with fruit or with cheese. To achieve a crusty exterior with a soft light texture inside, they need to be cooked quickly in a hot oven. Scones are best eaten on the day they are made, though they do freeze well. Serve plain scones, warm or cold and split with butter or thick cream and jam.

Makes 10

225g/8 oz self raising flour, plus extra
1 tsp baking powder
55g/2 oz butter
25g/1 oz caster sugar
1 medium egg, lightly beaten, plus extra for brushing
about 5 tbsp milk

1. Into a large bowl, sift the flour and baking powder. Using your fingertips, rub the butter into the flour until the mixture resembles fine crumbs. Stir in the sugar.

2. With a round flat knife, mix in the beaten egg and sufficient milk to make a soft dough. Turn out on to a lightly floured surface and knead lightly until smooth.

3. Roll out to about 1cm/½ in thick. With a 6.25cm/2½ in cutter, cut into circles (make sure that the cutter is floured and that you do not twist it as you cut through the dough), lightly re-rolling the trimmings as necessary.

4. Lightly dust a baking sheet with flour and put the scones on top. Brush the tops of the scones lightly with beaten egg.

5. Cook in a preheated oven at 220°C/425°F/Gas 7 for about 12 minutes or until well risen and golden brown.

6. Cool on a wire rack.

Fruit Scones

Follow the recipe for Scones. At the end of step 1, add 50g/1¾ oz dried fruit (sultanas or finely chopped ready-to-eat dried apricots or dates) and 25g/1 oz caster sugar.

Cheese Scones

Follow the recipe for Scones, omitting the sugar. At the end of step 1, add 50g/1¾ oz finely grated mature Cheddar cheese and ¾ tsp mustard powder. Serve warm, split and buttered.

Herb Scones

Follow the recipe for Scones, omitting the sugar. At the end of step 1, add 1 tbsp chopped fresh herbs (chives, parsley or thyme). Serve warm with soup or with cheese.

Shortbread

Scottish shortbread is believed to have been made as long ago as the 12th century. Always made with butter, it is a sweet, crumbly, melt-in-the-mouth biscuit which was usually served in triangles or 'Petticoat Tails'. These days, shortbread is eaten at any time of the year. Its strongest association still lies with Hogmanay, when first-footers are offered the biscuits in return for the good luck they bring to homes in the year ahead. It keeps well if stored in an airtight tin.

Makes 8 triangles

115g/4 oz soft butter
55g/2 oz caster sugar, plus extra for dusting
150g/5½ oz plain flour
25g/1 oz ground rice or semolina

1. Beat the butter and sugar together until light and fluffy. Sift in the flour and rice or semolina. Gradually stir them in, gathering the mixture together to form a dough.

2. Press the dough into an 18cm/7 in round flan ring on a baking sheet.

3. Prick well with a fork all over. With your finger and thumb, pinch the edges to make a pattern around the edge then, using a sharp knife, mark into 8 triangles.

4. Cook in a preheated oven at 170°C/325°F/Gas 3 for about 40 minutes or until pale golden brown.

5. Leave to stand for 5 minutes before cutting into triangles and dusting with caster sugar. Allow to cool completely on the baking sheet.

To microwave:

1. Follow step 1 above.

2. Line the base of an 18cm/7 in flan dish with baking paper.

3. Prick well with a fork all over.

4. Cook on MED-HIGH for 4-5 minutes or until the centre of the shortbread is just set.

5. Follow step 5 above.

Cornish or Devonshire Splits

Both Cornwall and Devon lay claim to these soft, light buns with their tops dusted with icing sugar. They are served split open to hold cream (clotted of course) and jam, treacle or golden syrup. You may hear them called 'chudleighs', 'tuffs' or, when served with cream and treacle, 'thunder and lightning'. Serve them hot, warm or cold, preferably on the day they are made (alternatively, they freeze well).

Makes about 14

450g/1 lb strong plain flour, plus extra if necessary
7g sachet easy-bake or easy-blend yeast
1 tsp sugar
300ml/½ pt lukewarm milk
1 tsp salt
50g/1¾ oz butter
icing sugar

1. Sift 115g/4 oz flour into a bowl and add the yeast and sugar. Stir in the lukewarm milk and leave to stand for about 30 minutes until frothy.
2. Into a large bowl, sift the remaining flour and the salt. Using your fingertips, rub the butter into the flour until the mixture resembles fine crumbs. Add the frothy yeast mixture and mix to a soft dough that leaves the sides of the bowl clean, adding a little extra flour if necessary.
3. Tip on to a lightly floured surface and knead until smooth and elastic.
4. Put into a clean bowl (warmed under the hot tap and dried), cover with oiled film and leave for about 1-1½ hours or until doubled in size.
5. Knock out the air and tip the dough on to a lightly floured surface. Divide the mixture into 14 equal-size pieces, then shape each one into a ball. Arrange them, about 1cm/½ in apart, on a lightly floured baking sheet.
6. Cover with oiled film and leave for about 40 minutes or until almost doubled in size.
7. Cook in a preheated oven at 220°C/425°F/Gas 7 for about 20 minutes until golden.
8. Sift over some icing sugar and leave to cool on a wire rack.

Mince Pies

Until the 1800s, these small pies with their rich, spicy filling would have included finely shredded fresh meat. Traditionally associated with Christmas, the pastry case is said to represent the crib in which Jesus lay and the spicy filling represents the exotic gifts presented to Him by the three wise men. Eating a mince pie on each of the 12 days of Christmas was supposed to guarantee happiness during the 12 months ahead.

The recipe below uses a slightly sweetened shortcrust pastry which is flavoured with finely grated lemon rind; you can, of course, use puff pastry. Buy a jar of good-quality mincemeat and, to make your mince pies really special, put a small spoonful of cream cheese or crème fraîche on top of the filling, before adding the pastry lid. Serve them warm with whipped cream, flavoured with a little brandy, rum or orange liqueur.

Makes 12

200g/7 oz plain flour
115g/4 oz chilled butter, cut into small cubes
25g/1 oz caster sugar
finely grated rind of 1 lemon
1 medium egg, beaten
350-450g/¾-1 lb mincemeat
milk
icing sugar

1. To make the pastry, sift the flour into a large bowl and add the butter. Using your fingertips, rub the butter into the flour until the mixture resembles fine crumbs (this can be done in a processor). Stir in the sugar and lemon rind, then add the egg, stirring until the mixture begins to cling together. Gather up the mixture to make a smooth firm dough. Wrap and chill for about 30 minutes to allow the pastry to 'relax'.

2. Roll out the pastry thinly and cut 12 rounds about 7.5cm/3 in across and 12 round lids about 6cm/2½ in across.

3. Use the larger rounds to line 12 greased patty tins. Spoon some mincemeat into each, making sure they are about half full. Brush the edges with water and top with a pastry lid, sealing well. Make a small slit in each lid. Brush the tops with milk.

4. Cook in a preheated oven at 220°C/425°F/Gas 7 for about 20 minutes until golden brown.

5. Leave to stand for 5 minutes before carefully transferring them to a wire rack. Sift over some icing sugar and leave to cool.

Eccles Cakes

These cakes, with a sweet and spicy fruit mixture in a case of crisp pastry, were first baked in the town of Eccles in Lancashire. No-one is quite sure of their origin, but it is thought they may have had a religious significance. You can, of course, make your own pastry, but it's quicker to use ready-made. Eccles Cakes are delicious when served warm.

Makes 8

25g/1 oz butter
115g/4 oz currants
25g/1 oz chopped mixed peel
50g/1¾ oz soft brown sugar
½ tsp ground mixed spice
225g/8 oz puff pastry, thawed if frozen
1 egg white, lightly beaten
caster sugar

1. Melt the butter and stir in the currants, peel, sugar and spice. Mix well.

2. On a lightly floured surface, roll out the pastry very thinly. Cut into 8 circles about 12.5cm/5 in across (use a saucer as a guide).

3. Spoon equal quantities of the fruit mixture into the centre of each circle. Brush the edges of the pastry with water, then draw up each one so that the pastry meets in the centre and completely encloses the fruit. Seal well and trim off any excess pastry.

4. Turn the cakes over and, with a rolling pin, roll gently until they are slightly flattened and the fruit just begins to show through the pastry. Brush with egg white and sprinkle with sugar. Make 3 long slits in the top of each cake. Arrange on a baking sheet.

5. Cook in a preheated oven at 220°C/425°F/Gas 7 for about 15 minutes until crisp and golden brown.

Potato Scones

Potato scones are traditional to Scotland and the North of England, where many people call them 'tattie scones'. In Ireland, they are called 'boxty pancakes' or 'boxty on the girdle' and would include self-raising flour instead of plain, milk instead of butter and half mashed potatoes and half grated raw potatoes (squeezed dry before adding to the mixture). Eat them warm, spread with butter and jam or serve them fried as part of a bacon-and-egg breakfast. Make sure you use floury potatoes, such as British grown Pentland Dell, King Edward or Maris Piper.

Makes about 10

450g/1 lb peeled potatoes (see above)
½ tsp salt
50g/1¾ oz butter
about 100g/3½ oz plain flour

1. Cook the potatoes in a pan of boiling salted water for about 20 minutes until soft and tender (alternatively, microwave with 4 tbsp water, covered, on HIGH for 8-10 minutes, stirring once, until tender). Drain and mash until very smooth.

2. Stir in the salt and butter, then enough flour to make a fairly stiff dough. Gather it into a smooth ball.

3. Turn on to a lightly floured surface and roll out to about 0.5cm/¼ in thick. Cut into 7.5cm/3 in rounds (or cut into triangles).

4. Cook on a preheated lightly-greased griddle or bakestone for 4-5 minutes on each side until golden brown (alternatively, use a heavy-based non-stick frying pan).

Boxty Bread

This Irish recipe is similar to the one for Boxty Pancakes or Potato Scones (page 149) – except it is cooked in the oven instead of on a griddle. The word boxty comes from *bochty* or *boch*, meaning 'poor' and, years ago, cooks would add potatoes to flour in order to make it go further. Boxty Bread is best made with floury potatoes, such as British-grown King Edward or Desirée. The freshly-cooked bread is delicious eaten warm with butter.

Makes 4 small loaves

675g/1½ lb peeled potatoes (see above)
25g/1 oz butter
150ml/¼ pt milk
salt and freshly ground black pepper
350g/12 oz self raising flour, plus extra if necessary
1 tsp baking powder

1. Cook half the potatoes in boiling salted water for 15-20 minutes until soft and tender (alternatively, microwave with 3 tbsp water, covered, on HIGH for about 8 minutes, stirring once, until tender). Drain and mash until very smooth. Stir in the butter.

2. Finely grate the remaining potatoes on to a clean tea towel. Roll up and squeeze well. Tip the potatoes into a large bowl and stir in the milk. Beat in the mashed potato and season well. Leave to cool slightly.

3. Sift the flour and baking powder over the potato mixture and mix to make a soft dough.

4. Turn out on to a lightly floured surface and knead until smooth (you may need to add a little extra flour if the dough is too soft). Quarter the dough, shape each piece into a small round loaf. Flatten slightly then, with a knife, cut a deep cross in the top of each. Put on to a greased baking sheet.

5. Cook in a preheated oven at 200°C/400°F/Gas 6 for about 35 minutes or until risen, golden brown and cooked through.

Soda Bread

In Ireland, Soda Bread is traditionally made with buttermilk. If you are able to buy some, use it in place of the yogurt and water. Best eaten on the day it is made, or toasted the day after. It's delicious with a bowl of hot soup or served as part of a "Ploughman's" lunch.

Makes 4 wedges

450g/1 lb plain white flour (or half white and half brown), plus extra for dusting
1 tbsp baking powder
1 tsp bicarbonate of soda
1 tsp salt
50g/1¾ oz butter
150ml/¼ pt natural yogurt

1. Preheat the oven to 220°C/425°F/Gas 7. Put a flat baking sheet inside to heat up.

2. Sift the flour, baking powder, bicarbonate of soda and salt into a large bowl. Using your fingertips, rub in the butter until the mixture resembles coarse crumbs.

3. Stir the yogurt into 225ml/8 fl oz water. Stir into the flour mixture, adding sufficient to make a soft dough. Turn on to a lightly floured surface and knead lightly until smooth. Shape into a ball and flatten the top slightly.

4. Put the dough on to the hot baking sheet, sift a little flour over the top and cut a cross in the top, about three-quarters of the way through.

5. Cook at 220°C/425°F/Gas 7 for about 30 minutes or until well risen and the crust is golden brown. When the bottom of the loaf is tapped, it should sound hollow.

6. Leave to cool before breaking into four wedges.

Hot Cross Buns

'Hot Cross Buns; Hot Cross Buns. One a penny, two a penny, Hot Cross Buns . . .' goes the rhyme. Here in Britain, these buns are traditionally eaten for breakfast on Good Friday. Though their true origin is unknown, the cross on the top of each bun is said to represent the Crucifixion and was thought to ward off evil spirits. In consequence, the buns developed into 'lucky charms' and would be hung in the corner of the kitchen. Serve them warm, split and buttered, or halved and toasted.

Makes 12

450g/1 lb strong plain flour, plus extra for kneading
½ tsp salt
2 tsp ground mixed spice
two 7g sachets easy-bake or easy-blend yeast
55g/2 oz caster sugar, plus 2 tbsp for glaze
115g/4 oz mixed dried fruit
300ml/½ pt milk
85g/3 oz butter
1 medium egg, beaten
50g/1¾ oz plain flour
beaten egg, for glazing

1. Sift the strong flour, salt and spice into a large bowl. Stir in the yeast, 55g/2 oz sugar and fruit. Put the milk and 55g/2 oz butter into a saucepan and heat gently until the butter just melts (the milk should be hand hot or tepid). Make a well in the flour mixture and add the milk and the egg. Mix to form a soft dough.

2. Turn on to a lightly floured surface and knead until smooth and elastic, adding a little extra flour if the dough is slightly sticky. Put into a clean bowl (warmed under the hot tap and dried), cover with oiled film and leave in a warm place for about 1 hour or until the dough has doubled its size.

3. Knock the air out of the dough and turn on to a lightly floured surface. Knead gently for a few minutes until smooth.

4. Divide the dough into 12 pieces and shape each one into a round. Arrange, about 1cm/½ in apart, on one or two greased baking sheet(s). Cover with oiled film and leave in a warm place for about 30 minutes or until doubled in size.

5. Meanwhile, make the pastry for the crosses. Sift the plain flour into a bowl and rub in the remaining 25g/1 oz butter until the mixture resembles fine crumbs. Stir in sufficient water to make a soft smooth dough. Roll out on a lightly floured surface cut into thin strips about 7.5cm/3 in long.

6. Lightly brush the risen buns with beaten egg, then lay two strips in a cross on top of each one.

7. Cook in a preheated oven at 200°C/400°F/Gas 6 for 15-20 minutes until well risen and golden brown.

8. Meanwhile, dissolve the remaining 2 tbsp caster sugar in 2 tbsp boiling water. As soon as the buns come out of the oven, lightly brush them with the sugar mixture.

9. Leave to cool on a wire rack before pulling the buns apart.

Border Tart

The original Scottish Border Tart would have been made from a yeast dough and filled with egg custard with added marzipan, almonds, citrus peel and dried fruit. These days, each recipe is likely to vary slightly from another. Here is the version which was proudly served to me, just north of the border, which my Scottish friends called Ecclefechan Butter Tart. I like to glaze the top with apricot jam, while others prefer to drizzle over some white glacé icing. Serve it at room temperature.

Serves 6

Pastry:
225g/8 oz plain flour
115g/4 oz butter or block margarine
25g/1 oz caster sugar
finely grated rind of 1 small orange
1 medium egg, lightly beaten

Filling:
85g/3 oz soft butter or margarine
85g/3 oz caster sugar
1 medium egg, lightly beaten
1 tsp vanilla extract
85g/3 oz self-raising flour
140g/5 oz mixed dried fruit
50g/1¾ oz glacé cherries, halved
2 tbsp apricot jam

1. To make the pastry, sift the flour into a large bowl and add the butter. Using your fingertips, rub the butter into the flour until the mixture resembles fine breadcrumbs (this can be done in a processor). Stir in the sugar, then add the orange rind and egg, stirring until the mixture begins to cling together. Gather up the mixture to make a firm dough. Wrap and chill for about 30 minutes to allow the pastry to 'relax'.

2. Roll out the pastry and use to line a 20cm/8 in flan tin, reserving any trimmings. With a fork, lightly prick the pastry all over. Line with baking paper and fill with baking beans.

3. Put the tin into a preheated oven and cook at 190°C/375°F/Gas 5 for 10 minutes. Carefully remove the paper and beans and continue to cook for 5-10 minutes or until lightly browned.

4. Meanwhile, prepare the filling. Beat the butter with the sugar until light and fluffy, then beat in the egg and vanilla extract. Sieve the flour over the top and, with a metal spoon, fold in gently. Stir in the dried fruit.

5. Spoon the filling into the pastry case and level the top. Roll out the pastry trimmings and, cut into thin strips and lay in a lattice pattern over the top. Arrange the cherry halves in the spaces between the pastry.

6. Put into the preheated oven and cook at 160°C/325°F/Gas 3 for about 40 minutes until set and golden brown. Leave to cool.

7. Put the jam into a small saucepan with 2 tbsp water. Heat gently until the jam has melted (this can easily be done in a small bowl in the microwave). If necessary, sieve to remove lumps. Brush the mixture over the cooled tart.

6

FEASTS FOR FESTIVITIES

We all love to celebrate high days and holidays. If food plays a major part in your revels (and it certainly does in our house), probably the first question you will ask yourself is 'what shall I serve?'. Listed below are some suggestions to help you to decide. Remember, they are only suggestions – there are plenty of other choices throughout the book. As well as several menus for specific occasions, I have listed events which are mentioned elsewhere in this book, with page numbers to take you to an appropriate (and traditional) recipe to celebrate the day.

Burns Night (January 25th)
Remembers and celebrates the birthday of Scotland's most famous poet, Robert Burns (1759-1796). To start, serve **Cock-a-Leekie Soup** (page 12). Follow either with the traditional haggis (cut it open by marking the cross of St Andrew in the top) and bashed neeps (mashed turnips) and tatties (potatoes) or with **Venison Casserole** (page 78) and **Clapshot** (page 42). Finish with **Whim Wham** (page 104).

St Valentine's Day (February 14th)

The day for celebrating lovers, when the custom is to send (anonymous) greetings cards or gifts to declare affection for a chosen partner. Celebrate also by sharing a meal. Halve the recipes to serve 2. Why not serve delicate **Potted Salmon** (page 29), then **Duck with Cumberland Sauce** (page 77)? Finish with a deliciously silky **Syllabub** (page 105).

St David's Day (March 1st)

Celebrates the patron saint of Wales with the wearing of leeks and daffodils on the country's national day. I usually serve **Leek Soup** or *Cawl Cennin* (page 16) to start and follow with **Lamb with Honey and Herbs** (page 55) accompanied with **Punchnep** (page 43). No dessert, but serve **Welsh Cakes** (page 130) with the coffee.

St Patrick's Day (March 17th)

Ireland's national holiday celebrates its patron saint, St Patrick, whose alleged use of the shamrock as an illustration of the Trinity led to its being regarded as the Irish national emblem. Start the meal with **Potato Soup with Parsley** (page 14). An appropriate main course would be **Beef in Stout** (page 93) served with **Colcannon** (page 49) or wedges of freshly-baked **Soda Bread** (page 151). Finish with a **Fruit Fool** (page 102).

St George's Day (April 23rd)

Is England's festival day to celebrate its patron saint, St George, who is linked to many legends, the most popular of which relates his encounter with the dragon. For starters, serve mini portions of **Bubble and Squeak** (page 37) with a salad garnish. For the main course, offer **Roast Beef with Yorkshire Pudding and Gravy** (page 56) and end with a traditional **Apple Pie** (page 96).

St Andrew's Day (November 30th)

Is the feast day of the patron saint of Scotland, St Andrew, who was one of the 12 apostles of Jesus Christ. Begin by serving bowls of **Cullen Skink** (page 24). **Pheasant Casserole** (page 82) would make a wonderful main course and **Butterscotch Tart** (page 111) a delicious dessert. Make sure you offer your guests a drink of 'the water of life' (whisky, of course).

Easter Sunday (date varies)
Is the annual festival commemorating the resurrection of Jesus
Christ, and the principal feast of the Christian year. It is celebrated
on a Sunday on varying dates between March 22 and April 25.
Kipper or Smoked Mackerel Pâté (page 26) would make a
suitable starter, followed by **Crown Roast of Lamb or Guard of
Honour** (page 58), using the new season's lamb. Serve **Pond
Pudding** (page 122) for dessert. And do remember to make a
Simnel Cake (page 132) for afternoon tea.

Christmas Day (December 25th)
The annual festival celebrating the birth of Jesus Christ in Bethlehem
as related in the Gospels of Matthew and Luke. Today, Christmas is
as much a wordly festival as a religious one. It is a time for giving
presents, family reunions and, in the British Isles, a traditional
Christmas meal. Start by serving **Potted Shrimps** (page 29) then
follow with the classic dishes of **Roast Turkey with Stuffing and
Sauce** (page 70) and **Christmas Pudding** (page 112). Offer your
guests **Mince Pies** (page 146) with their coffee.

Bonfire/Guy Fawkes Night, see page 135.

Good Friday, see page 152.

Harvest Time, see page 76.

Halloween, see page 49.

Michaelmas, see page 68.

Mothering Sunday, see page 132.

New Year, see pages 118 and 144.

Shrove Tuesday, see page 107.

INDEX